IQ
Puzzles

IQ Puzzles

Compiled by Joe Cameron

Sterling Publishing Co., Inc.
New York

Library of Congress Cataloging-in-Publication Data Available

10 9 8 7 6 5 4 3 2 1

Published by Sterling Publishing Co., Inc.
387 Park Avenue South, New York, NY 10016

© Arcturus Publishing Limited

First Sterling Edition Published in 2003

Manufactured in China

ISBN 1-4027-0963-3

IQ
Puzzles

Welcome to **IQ Puzzles**, a collection of over 500 puzzles to challenge and test your mental agility and problem-solving powers.

The book is divided up into twenty levels of ascending difficulty - the first chapters being easier than the last ones. Each level is clearly marked down the side of the page and is better to work through in a methodical order and resist the temptation to flick through at random. If you find the first few chapters easy, please be patient and use them as a warm-up excercise for the more challenging puzzles later on.

When you finish each chapter take time to study the answers and go back over the questions until you fully understand the logic behind them. You will find, as you progress through the book, that there are certain mathematical patterns that seem to re-occur or visual clues that overlap. These can help but, and you must be warned, just when you think you can recognise a pattern it changes!

Think laterally, don't just look at the obvious, look at the puzzles from all angles. The rewards can be hours and hours of fun.

Over the page we have listed a few tables which you might find helpful. These contain some basic mathematical formulas to help you do battles with the puzzles.

Good luck and enjoy!

Numerical values

Letter	Value	Value
A	1	26
B	2	25
C	3	24
D	4	23
E	5	22
F	6	21
G	7	20
H	8	19
I	9	18
J	10	17
K	11	16
L	12	15
M	13	14
N	14	13
O	15	12
P	16	11
Q	17	10
R	18	9
S	19	8
T	20	7
U	21	6
V	22	5
W	23	4
X	24	3
Y	25	2
Z	26	1

Multiplication Table

×	1	2	3	4	5	6	7	8	9	10	11	12
1	1	2	3	4	5	6	7	8	9	10	11	12
2	2	4	6	8	10	12	14	16	18	20	22	24
3	3	6	9	12	15	18	21	24	27	30	33	36
4	4	8	12	16	20	24	28	32	36	40	44	48
5	5	10	15	20	25	30	35	40	45	50	55	60
6	6	12	18	24	30	36	42	48	54	60	66	72
7	7	14	21	28	35	42	49	56	63	70	77	84
8	8	16	24	32	40	48	56	64	72	80	88	96
9	9	18	27	36	45	54	63	72	81	90	99	108
10	10	20	30	40	50	60	70	80	90	100	110	120
11	11	22	33	44	55	66	77	88	99	110	121	132
12	12	24	36	48	60	72	84	96	108	120	132	144

Prime Numbers

2
3
5
7
11
13
17
19
23
29

Square and Cube Numbers

	Square Numbers	Cube Numbers
1	1	1
2	4	8
3	9	27
4	16	64
5	25	125
6	36	216
7	49	343
8	64	512
9	81	729
10	100	1000
11	121	1331
12	144	1728
13	169	2197
14	196	2744
15	225	3375
16	256	4096
17	289	4913
18	324	5832
19	361	6859
20	400	8000

PUZZLE 1

Which number replaces the blank and completes the sequence?

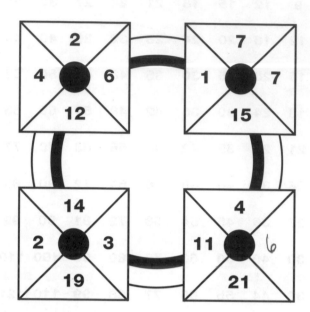

PUZZLE 2

Which letter replaces the blank and completes the puzzle?

PUZZLE 3

Which number is missing from the chain?

PUZZLE 4

Which number goes in the empty box?

Which letter completes the third circle?

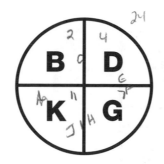
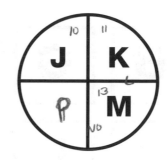

Which number goes in the empty box?

Remove three matches to leave just three squares.

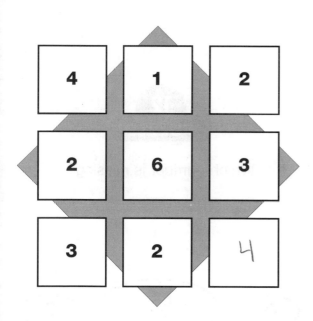

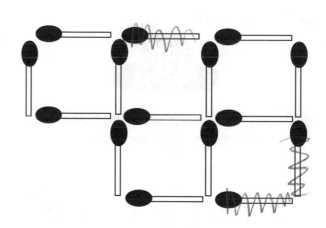

Which letter follows next?

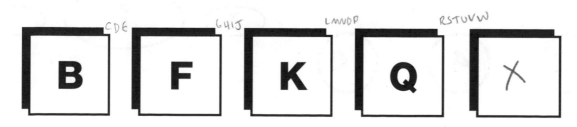

LEVEL 1

9

PUZZLE 9

Which letter goes in the empty square?

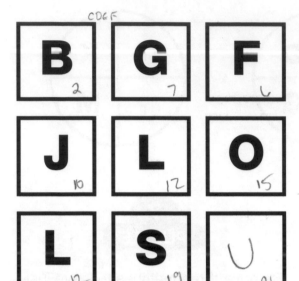

B	G	F
J	L	O
L	S	U

PUZZLE 10

Following a logical pattern, complete this puzzle.

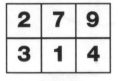

5	3	8
4	9	13

2	7	9
3	1	4

3	6	9
7	1	8

PUZZLE 11

Which number replaces the blank and completes the sequence?

7 2 9

9 3 12

12 4 16

PUZZLE 12

Which number is missing?

3 9 3

5 7 1

7 1

PUZZLE 13

Which number replaces the blank and completes the sequence?

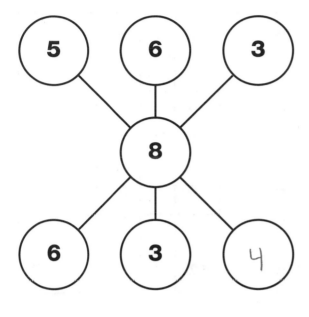

PUZZLE 14

Which number is missing from this sequence?

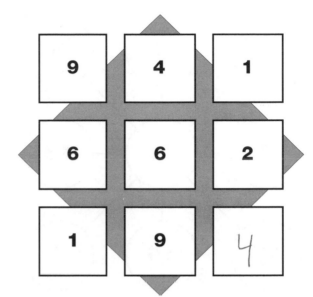

PUZZLE 15

Draw the face in the empty box which continues this pattern.

PUZZLE 16

Which number goes in the empty circle?

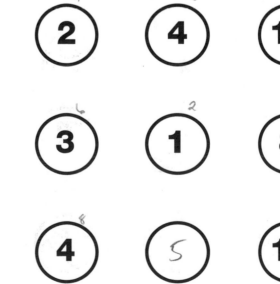

PUZZLE 17

Which number completes the puzzle?

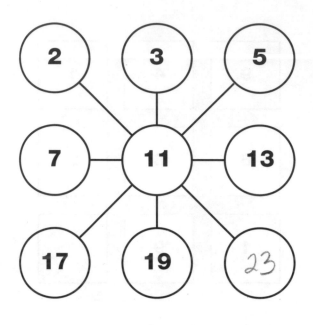

PUZZLE 18

Which number replaces the question mark in the bottom square?

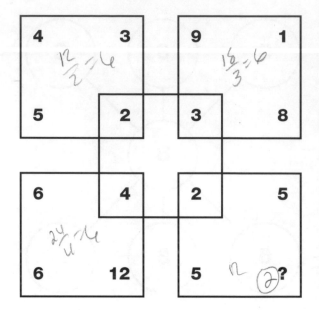

PUZZLE 19

Which letter is the odd one out in each shape?

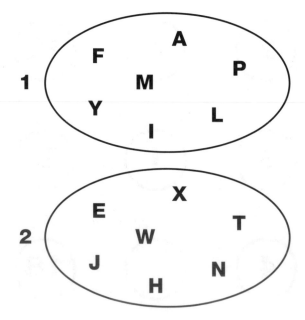

PUZZLE 20

Which number is missing from the empty segment?

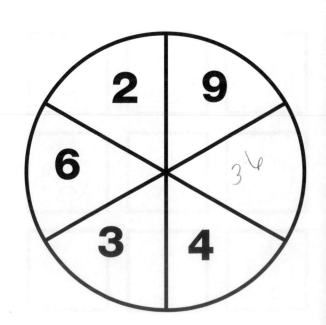

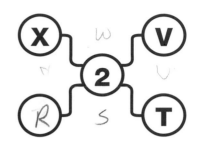

PUZZLE 21

What is missing from the last grid?

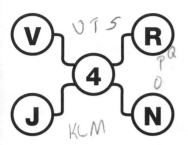

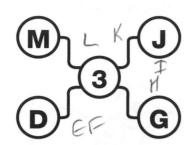

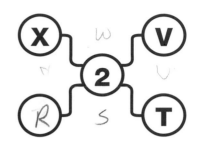

PUZZLE 22

Can you work out which letter is missing?

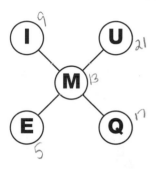

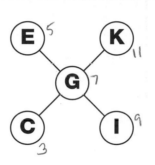

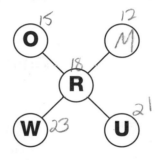

PUZZLE 23

Enter the correct number into the empty square.

4	9	20
8	5	14
10	3	

PUZZLE 24

Following a logical pattern, complete this puzzle.

1	5	7	13
15	5	4	6
3	8	2	13
12	5	2	5

By following this series of cogs attached to the float, can you work out if the flood warning works correctly?

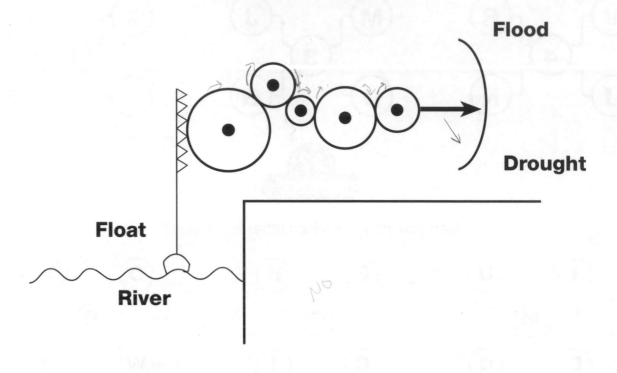

Flood

Drought

Float

River

PUZZLE 26

Which letter replaces the blank and completes the sequence?

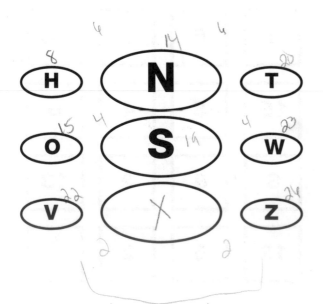

PUZZLE 27

What is missing from the empty segment of the wheel?

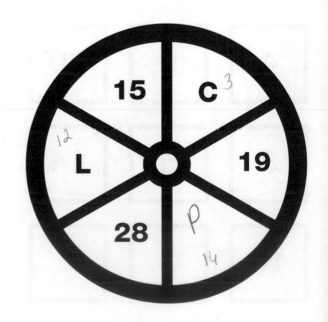

Which playing card completes the sequence?

Which two letters are missing?

A	W
C	U
E	S
G	Q
I	O
K	M

Draw the dot in the correct segment of the last circle.

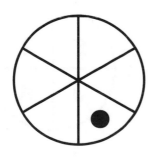 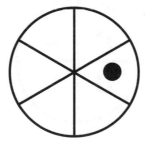 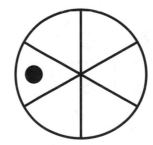

  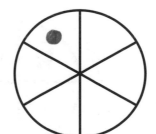

LEVEL 1

15

PUZZLE 31

Which number is missing from the third circle?

PUZZLE 32

Complete the last star.

PUZZLE 33

Which two letters will complete this puzzle?

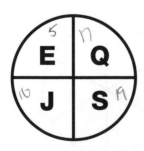

34 PUZZLE

Which number is missing?

3   5   2

6   11   5

2   9   7

35 PUZZLE

Which number fits into the empty link?

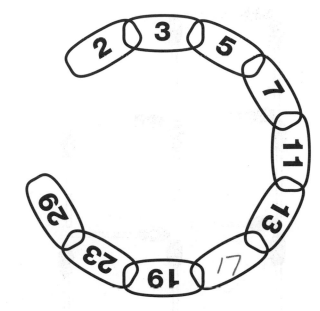

2 3 5 7 11 13 17 19 23 29

36 PUZZLE

Which letter completes the sequence?

 K 11   Q 17   F 6

R 18   Y 25   G 7

M 13   B 2   K 11

O 15   E 5   J 10

37 PUZZLE

Which number goes in the centre?

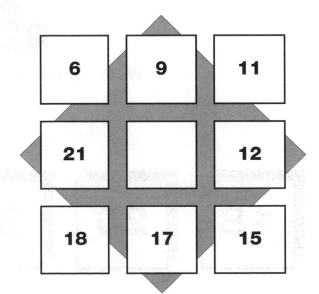

6	9	11
21		12
18	17	15

PUZZLE 1

Remove two matches to leave just four squares.

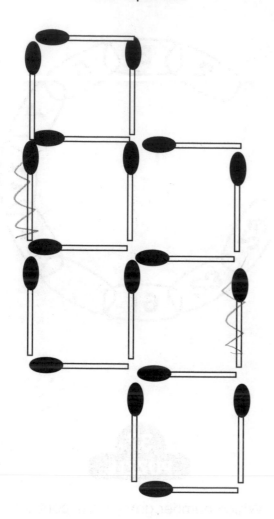

PUZZLE 2

If the bottom cog is turned anticlockwise will the flag at the top be raised or lowered?

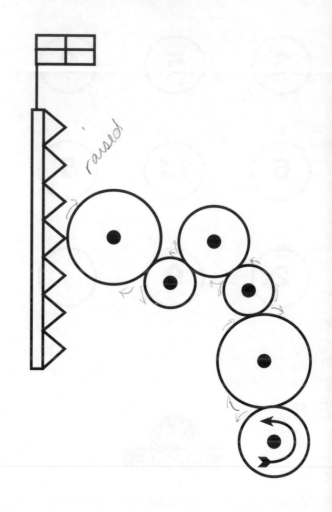

raised

PUZZLE 3

Which number continues this sequence?

18   20   24   32   48

2   4   8   16

PUZZLE 4

Which number will complete this teaser?

10 ^{2} 8 ^{2} 6

3 ^{4} 7 ^{4} 11

2   *3*   4

PUZZLE 5

Which letter goes into the last square of the bottom grid?

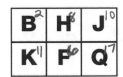

B^2	H^6	J^{10}
K^{11}	F^6	Q^7

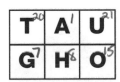

T^{20}	A^1	U^{21}
G^7	H^8	O^{15}

L^{12}	N^{14}	Z^{24}
R^{18}	C^3	*U* ^{21}

PUZZLE 6

Which number is missing from the box?

8	3	4
1	5	*9*
6	7	2

PUZZLE 7

Fill in the final box to complete the sequence.

4   23 =27

D	W

2	7

21 12   =33

U	L

3	3

7   15   =22

G	O

2	*2*

20

PUZZLE 8

Which letter is missing from the last star?

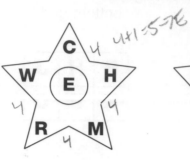

4 4+1=5=7E

C
W (E) H
4   4
R   M
4

E 8
O (I) N
       8
F   W
6

A 6
C (G) H
V   O

PUZZLE 9

Which letter replaces the blank and completes the sequence?

D⁴

P¹⁶

B²

N¹⁴

Z

PUZZLE 10

Which letter goes in the empty circle?

Q | J 10 | D 4
C 3 | K 11 | N 14
T 20 | U 21 | R 18

PUZZLE 11

Which number completes the last triangle?

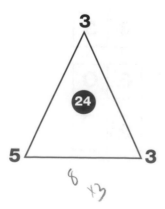

3
(24)
5   3
8 ×3

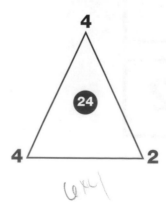

4
(24)
4   2
6×4/

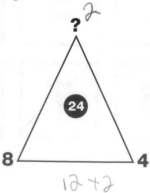

? 2
(24)
8   4
12+2

PUZZLE 12

Following a logical sequence, can you complete this puzzle?

8 / 2 = 4

5	13	4
6	10	2

4 / 2 = 2

16 / 2 = 8

3	19	8
6	20	7

14 / 2

PUZZLE 13

Which letter replaces the question mark?

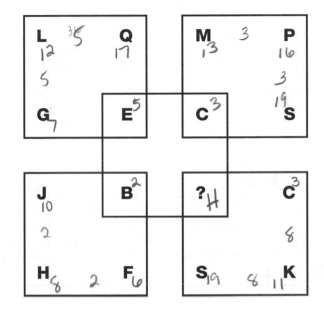

L 3 5 / 12 / 5   Q 17
M 3 / 13   P 16 / 3 / 19
G 7   E 5   C 3   S
J 10 / 2   B 2   ? H   C 3 / 8
H 8   2   F 6   S 19   8   11   K

PUZZLE 14

Fill in the empty box.

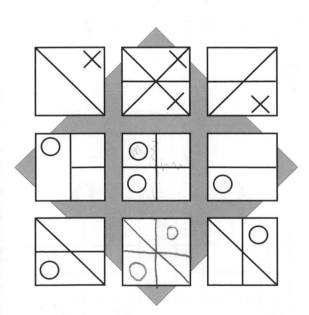

PUZZLE 15

Which number completes this sequence?

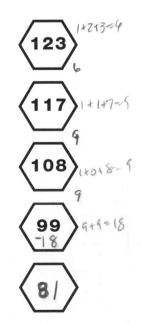

123   1+2+3=6
6
117   1+1+7=9
9
108   1+0+8=9
9
99   9+9=18
-18
81

LEVEL 2

Which of the four squares at the bottom completes the pattern?

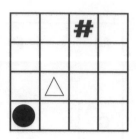
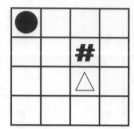
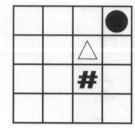
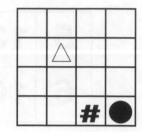

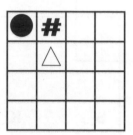
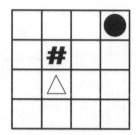
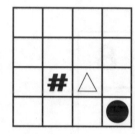
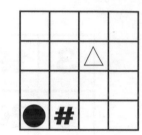

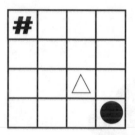
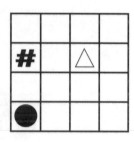
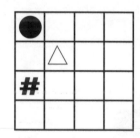
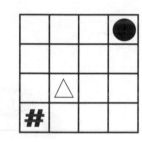

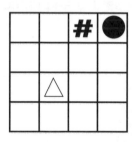
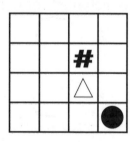
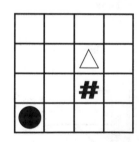

?

A
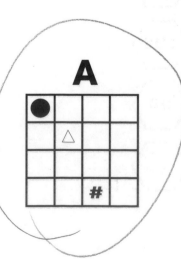

B
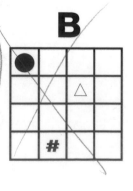

C
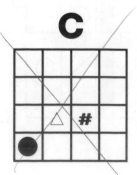

D
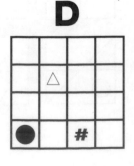

LEVEL

2

Which number completes this puzzle?

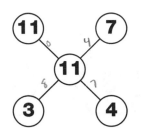 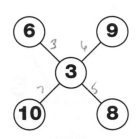 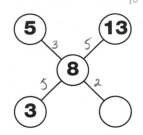

Which pattern completes the grid?

1   **2**   **3**   **4**   **5**

Which number is missing?

LEVEL

2

23

PUZZLE 20

Using every number between 1 and 9, fill in the spaces on this triangle so that the numbers on each side add up to 20.

PUZZLE 21

Which number is missing?

PUZZLE 22

Which number is missing from the third wheel?

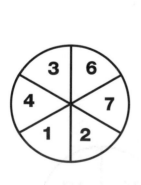
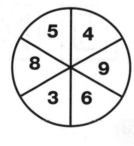

PUZZLE 23

Which number goes in the empty segment?

24 PUZZLE

Sean caught a prize fish last weekend. He was going to measure it but realised that his ruler was not long enough. He was able to measure the head and discovered that it was 9cm long, he then measured the tail and found that it was the length of the head plus half the length of the body. if the body was the length of the head plus the tail, what is the total length of the fish?

$b = h + t$

$b = 9 + 9 + \frac{1}{2}b$

$\frac{1}{2}b = 18$

$b = 36$

$9 + 36 + 9 + \frac{1}{2} \times 36 = 72$

25 PUZZLE

Which number completes the chain?

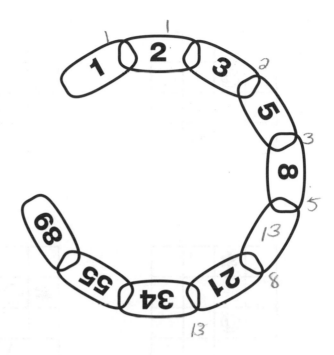

26 PUZZLE

Which letter replaces the blank and completes the sequence?

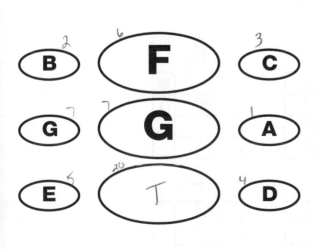

B   F   C

G   G   A

E   T   D

27 PUZZLE

Which number logically goes in the centre of this puzzle?

3   11   19

5   13   23

7   17   29

Which of the bottom six grids completes this pattern?

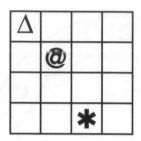

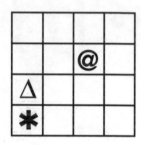

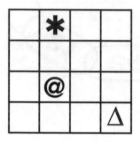

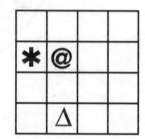

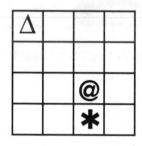

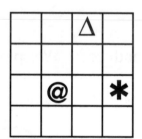

?

A

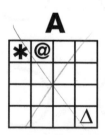

B

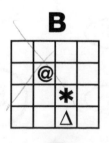

C

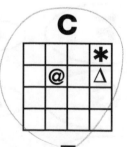

D

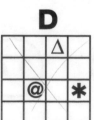

E

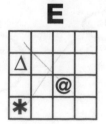

F

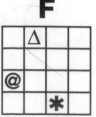

PUZZLE 29

Which number is missing?

PUZZLE 30

Which letter goes in the empty segment?

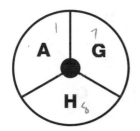
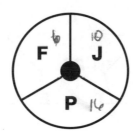
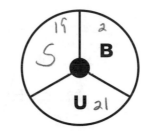

PUZZLE 31

Which letter replaces the blank and completes the sequence?

PUZZLE 32

Which letter completes this puzzle?

PUZZLE 1

Which letter tops the third triangle?

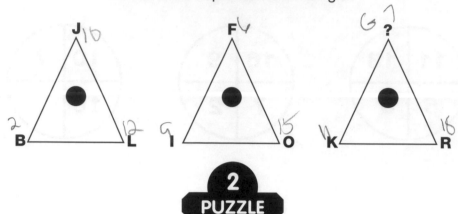

J 10
B 2   L 12

F ✓
I 9   O 15

G ↗ ?
K 4   R 18

PUZZLE 2

Which number goes in the third star?

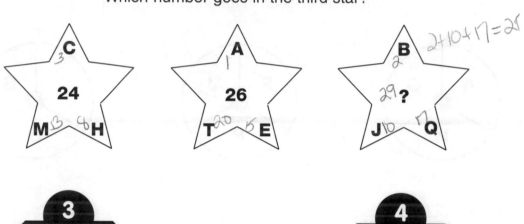

C 3
24
M 13   8 H

A 1
26
T 20   5 E

B 2   2+10+17=2r
29 ?
J 10   17 Q

PUZZLE 3

Which letter replaces the blank and completes the sequence?

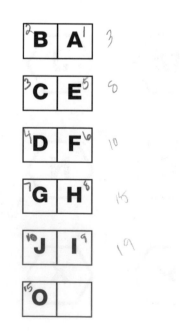

2 B	A 1	3
3 C	E 5	8
4 D	F 6	10
7 G	H 8	15
10 J	I 9	19
15 O		

PUZZLE 4

If two painters can complete two rooms in two hours, how many painters would it take to do 18 rooms in 6 hours?

2 painters
2 rooms
2 hours

18 rooms
6 hours

6 painters

PUZZLE 5

Which letter goes in the empty segment?

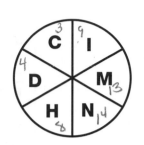

PUZZLE 6

Which number links all these?

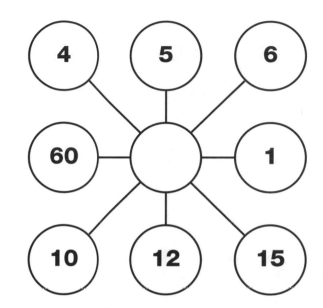

PUZZLE 7

Which number logically finishes this puzzle?

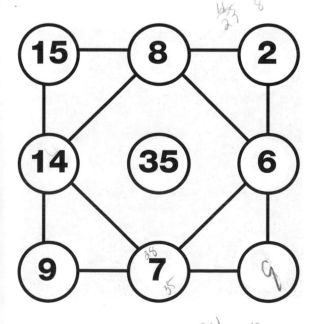

PUZZLE 8

Which number replaces the question mark?

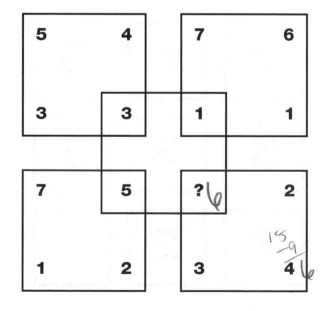

LEVEL

3

9 PUZZLE

Which number goes in the empty circle?

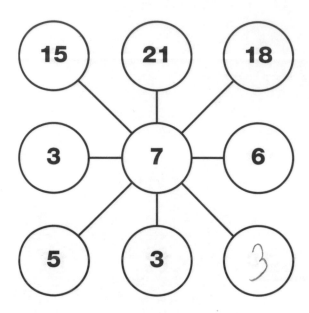

15 21 18

3 7 6

5 3 3

10 PUZZLE

Which number completes this sequence?

2	5
7	3
10	4
14	6
20	8
28	12

11 PUZZLE

Which number finishes this grid?

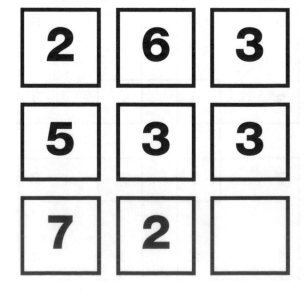

2	6	3
5	3	3
7	2	

12 PUZZLE

Which letter replaces the blank and completes the sequence?

B 2   C 3   E 5

G 7   K 11   M 13

Q 17   S 19   W 23

prime #s

13 PUZZLE

Which playing card is missing?

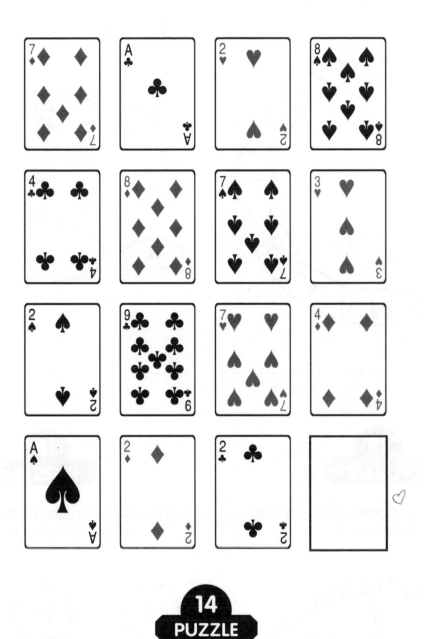

14 PUZZLE

Which character is missing from the point in the last star?

15 PUZZLE

Which letter goes in the final link to complete the chain?

16 PUZZLE

Which number finishes this puzzle?

17 PUZZLE

Which number goes in the empty segment?

18 PUZZLE

Which letter replaces the blank and completes the sequence?

Which number goes in the middle of the last triangle?

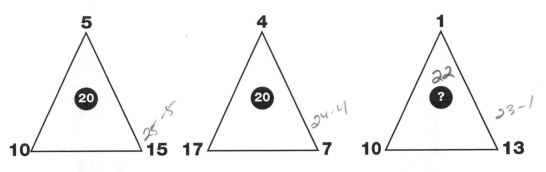

5

20

10   15   25-15

4

20

17   7   24-4

1

22
?

10   13   23-1

Which number completes the chain?

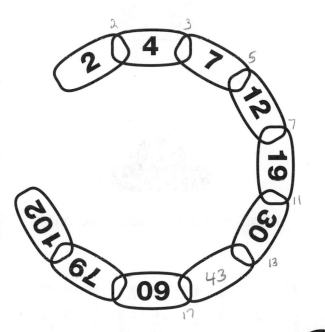

2   4   7   12   19   30   09   79   102

2   3   5   7   11   13   43   17

Which letter replaces the blank and completes the wheel?

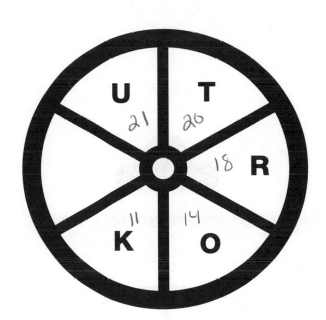

U   T   R   K   O

21   26   18   11   14

Which number goes in the blank segment of the last circle?

14   3   10

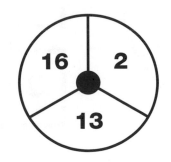

16   2   13

10   7   2

LEVEL

3

33

Which number goes in the empty circle?

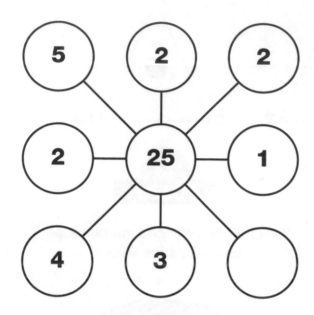

Which character logically completes this sequence?

B	A
2	8

J	N
2	3

Q	K
3	

25 PUZZLE

Which letter goes in the empty segment?

26 PUZZLE

Which number will finish this grid?

5	8	12
7	12	18
3	4	

Which number does not fit in this sequence?

1 - 2 - 3 - 6 - 7 - 8 - 14 - 15 - 30

Which number is the odd one out in each shape?

Which number is missing from the puzzle?

A
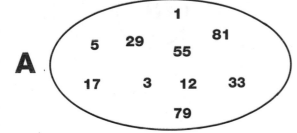

B
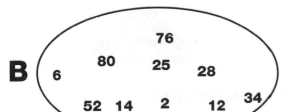

Which number is missing in the last grid?

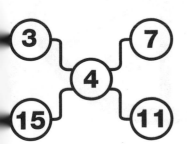

LEVEL

3

35

Which letter replaces the blank and completes the sequence?

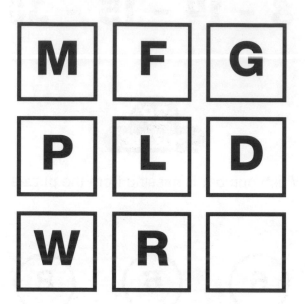

M	F	G
P	L	D
W	R	

Which letter goes in the empty circle and completes this puzzle?

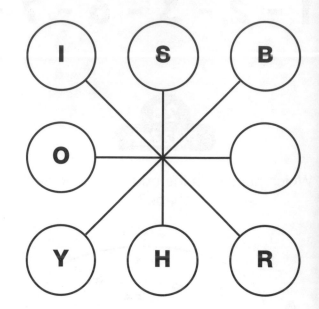

Jacob is 12 years old. He is 3 times as old as his brother. How old will Jacob be when he is twice as old?

Which number goes in the empty segment and completes the wheel?

35 PUZZLE

Which number goes in the empty square?

J	F	N
8	4	0

B	G	P
2	2	4

O	D	I
5	4	

36 PUZZLE

Which number goes in the empty circle and finishes the puzzle?

4   6   2

7   8   1

1   4   ( )

37 PUZZLE

Which character is missing from this puzzle?

B	I
W	P

D	J
V	P

A	F
P	K

J	N
V	R

N	
W	T

LEVEL

PUZZLE 1

Which letter replaces the blank and completes the sequence?

 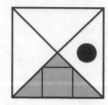 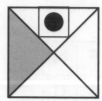

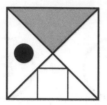 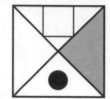 

A **B** **C** **D** **E** **F**

PUZZLE 2

Which number goes in the empty square?

3	7	10
4	11	15
6	4	

PUZZLE 3

Which number completes the sequence?

G	M
2	0
N	T
3	4
U	B
2	

Draw the correct pattern in the empty box to complete the pattern.

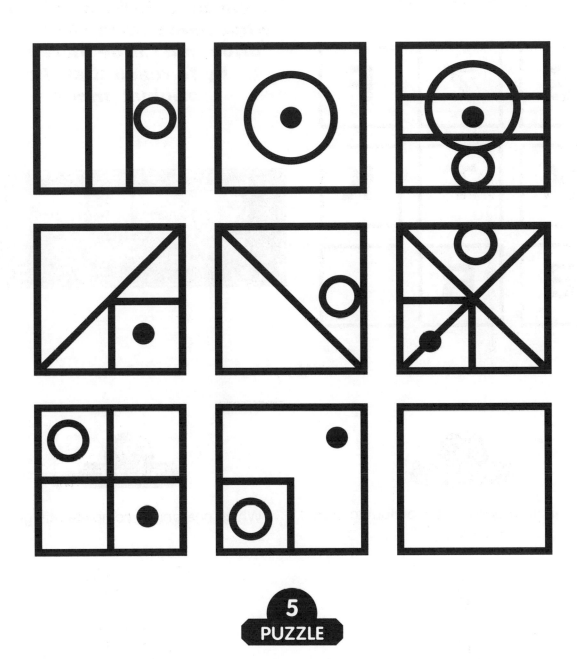

Which number goes in the empty circle?

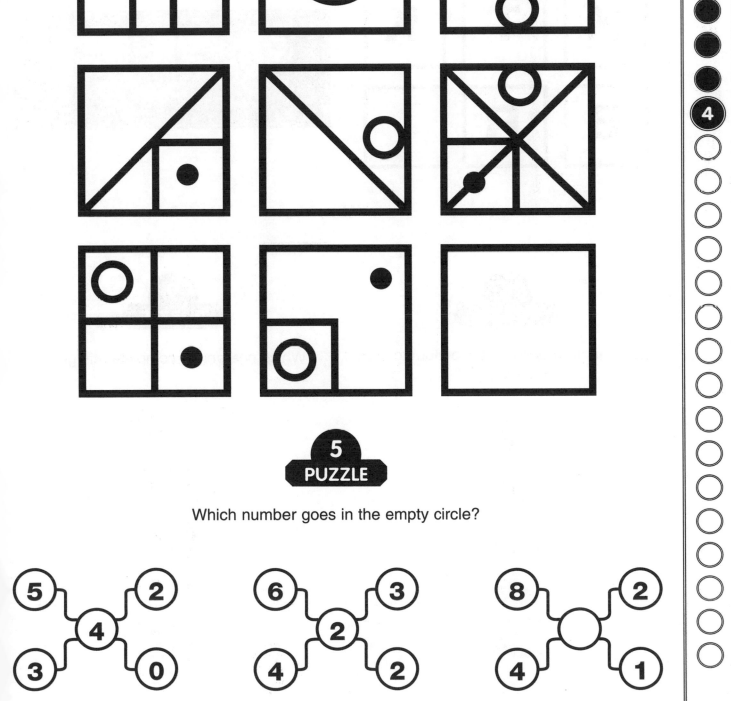

PUZZLE 6

Which letter replaces the blank and completes the sequence?

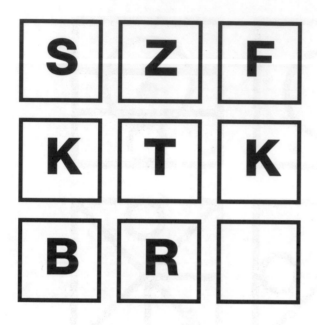

S	Z	F
K	T	K
B	R	

PUZZLE 7

If the price of a dress was cut by 20% for a sale, by what percentage of the sale price must it be increased by to resell it at the original price?

PUZZLE 8

Which number goes at the bottom to start the sequence?

6

11

15

18

20

PUZZLE 9

Which characters complete this grid?

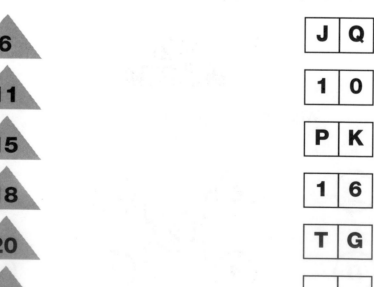

J	Q
1	0
P	K
1	6
T	G

Which of the bottom numbers goes in the centre circle?

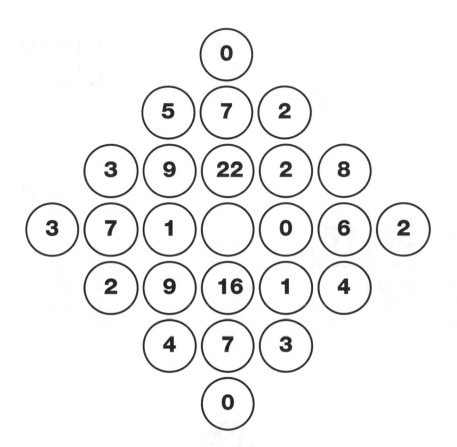

0

5 7 2

3 9 22 2 8

3 7 1 ( ) 0 6 2

2 9 16 1 4

4 7 3

0

13 15 17 19 21 23 25 27

Which letter finishes off the third triangle?

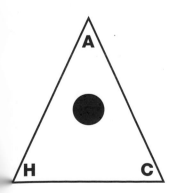
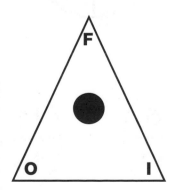
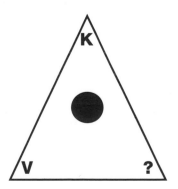

12 PUZZLE

Which number is missing from the bottom grid?

4	15	6
7	27	11

6	33	16
3	12	

13 PUZZLE

Which letter logically completes the last box of letters?

H	X	O
Q	A	J

Z	R	K
F	N	U

S	G	D
A	M	

14 PUZZLE

Which number goes in the empty segment?

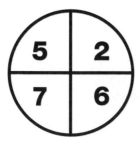

PUZZLE 15

Which letter replaces the blank and completes the third wheel?

 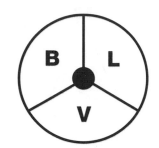 

PUZZLE 16

Which number replaces the blank and completes the sequence?

4	5	6	10
4	3	3	2
4	5	6	0
11	7	6	

PUZZLE 17

George has a square plot of land, but the corner of his house takes up 1/4 of the available space as the picture shows. He wants to divide the remaining space into 4 equal plots, of the same area and basic shape. It was difficult   to do as the plots were not arranged in the most practical way but can you work out how George managed it?

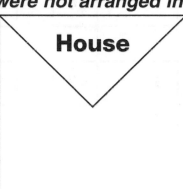

House

PUZZLE 18

Which letter replaces the blank and completes the sequence?

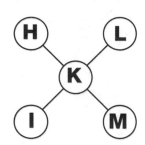 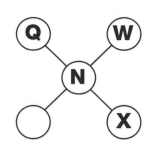

LEVEL

4

43

19 PUZZLE

Which number is missing from the last triangle?

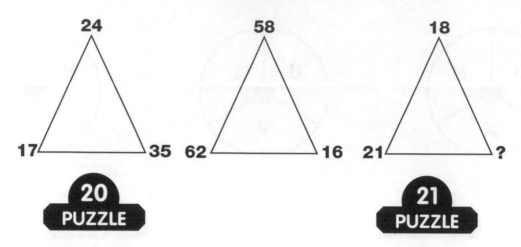

20 PUZZLE

Which number replaces the question mark?

21 PUZZLE

Which playing card is missing from this puzzle?

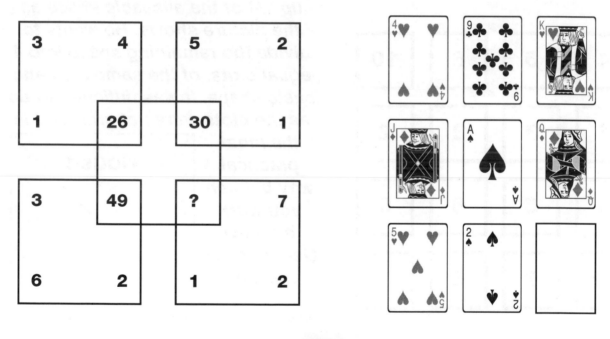

22 PUZZLE

Which letter replaces the question mark and completes the sequence?

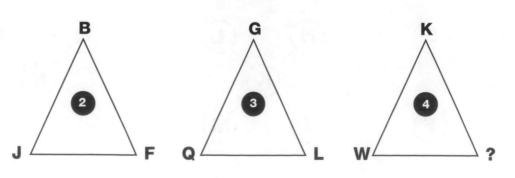

PUZZLE 23

If it takes 2 garage mechanics 3 hours to repair 6 cars, how many mechanics would it take to repair 22 cars in 5 hours?

PUZZLE 24

What is the fewest number of matches that need to be moved in order to make the fish swim in the opposite direction?

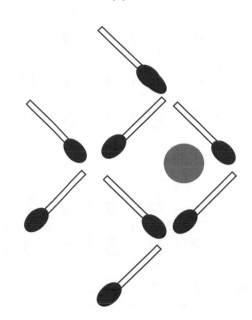

PUZZLE 25

Which number should appear at the bottom of this pile?

11
12
14
18
26

PUZZLE 26

Which number goes in the empty segment?

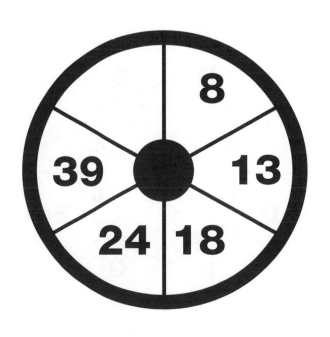

8
13
18
24
39

PUZZLE 27

Which number is missing?

3	4	7	2	9	3
2	2	1	9	1	6
5	6	9	2	0	9

1	7	8	6	3	2
4	3	2	8	1	1
6	1	1	4	4	

PUZZLE 28

Move just 4 matches to make 3 equilateral triangles.

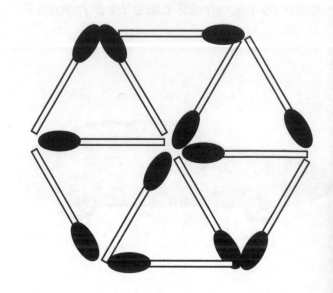

PUZZLE 29

Which letter is missing from the web?

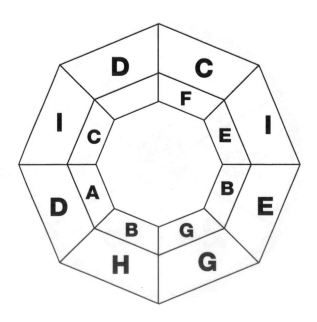

PUZZLE 30

Which letter is the odd one out in each shape?

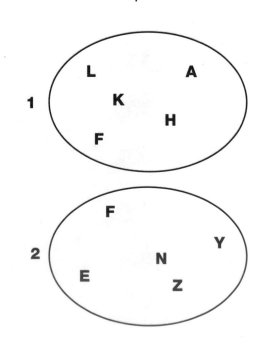

PUZZLE 1

Gill's puppy was growing fast. In the first five days since she got it it had eaten 100 dog biscuits. If each day it had eaten 6 more than the previous day, how many biscuits had it eaten on the first day?

PUZZLE 2

Which two numbers continue this sequence?

1 - 10 - 3 - 9 - 5 - 8 - 7 - 7 - 9 - 6 - ? - ?

PUZZLE 3

Which number follows on from these three?

PUZZLE 4

Which letter goes in the middle of the third triangle?

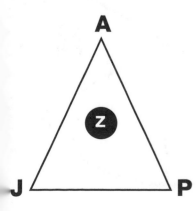
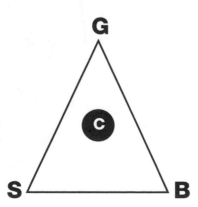
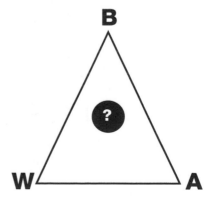

47

PUZZLE 5

Which number continues this sequence?

| 6 | 10 | 18 | 34 | |

PUZZLE 6

Which number is missing from the last puzzle?

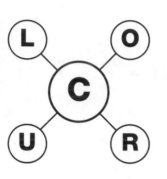
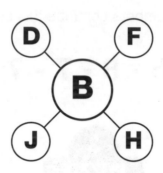
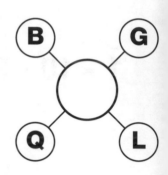

PUZZLE 7

Which number replaces the blank and completes the sequence?

1	1
2	1
3	2
5	3
8	5
	8

PUZZLE 8

Which letter is missing from the empty segment?

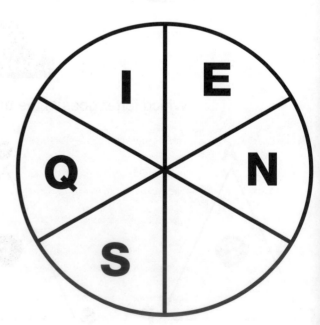

PUZZLE 9

Which number goes in the blank link and completes the chain?

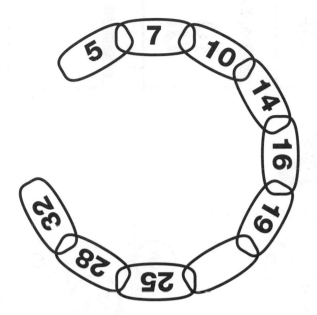

5 7 10 14 16 19 25 28 32

PUZZLE 10

Which number replaces the question mark?

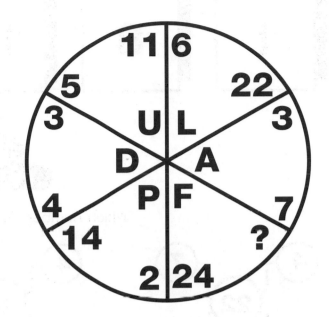

11 | 6
5 | 22
3 | 3
U | L
D | A
P | F
4 | 7
14 | ?
2 | 24

PUZZLE 11

Which letter is missing?

B	D	G
D	O	K
T	A	P
K	C	

PUZZLE 12

Alex is crossing the desert with his dog, Lucky. He starts off with a full waterbottle and drinks 1/3 of the contents during the first day. He then lets Lucky drink half of what is left. The next day, Alex drinks a 1/4 of what has been saved from the previous day. What fraction of the original amount did he save for Lucky?

Which number continues this sequence?

1	8	16	25	

Which number fills the empty circle?

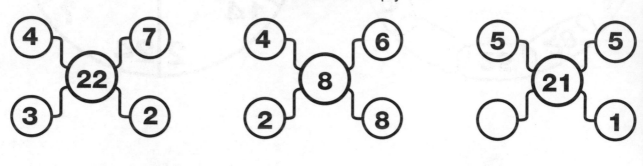

4   7
22
3   2

4   6
8
2   8

5   5
21
◯   1

Here is a set of cogs connected via drive belts. If the top left cog is turned clockwise will all the cogs turn freely?

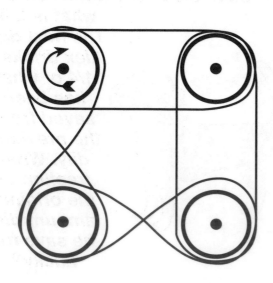

Which number goes in the empty square?

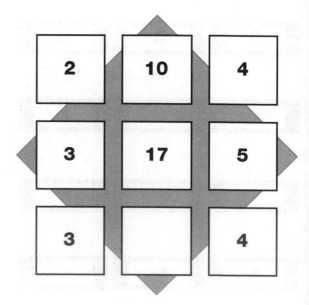

2	10	4
3	17	5
3		4

LEVEL

5

Which number fills the empty segment?

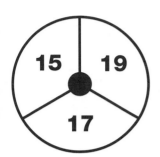
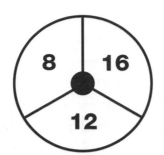

Which of the bottom squares fits logically with the pattern?

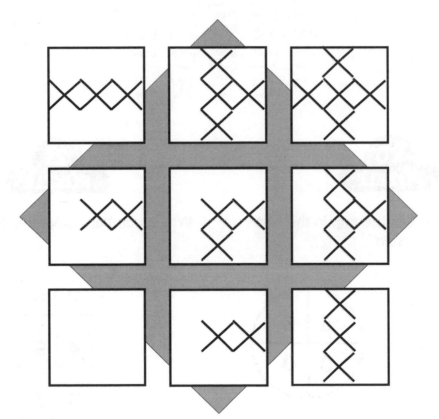

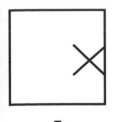
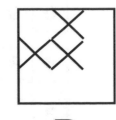
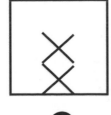
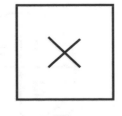

A   **B**   **C**   **D**   **E**

LEVEL

5

PUZZLE 19

Which watch fits on the end of this sequence?

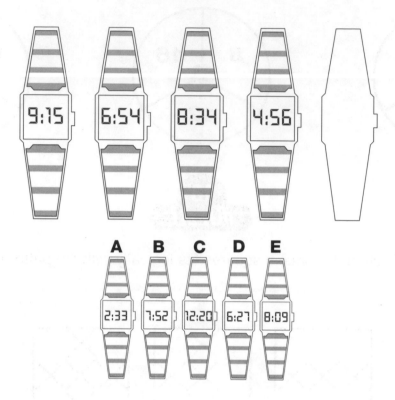

PUZZLE 20

Which number fills the gap in the last circle?

PUZZLE 21

Which number completes this puzzle?

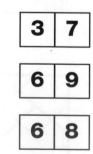

Which of the bottom shapes fits on the end of the top line?

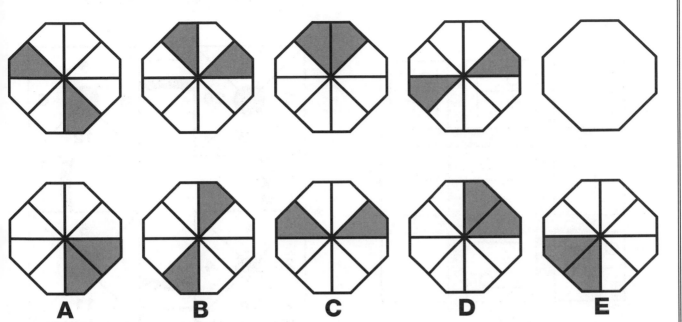

A   B   C   D   E

Fill in the empty segment to complete the puzzle.

Which number is missing?

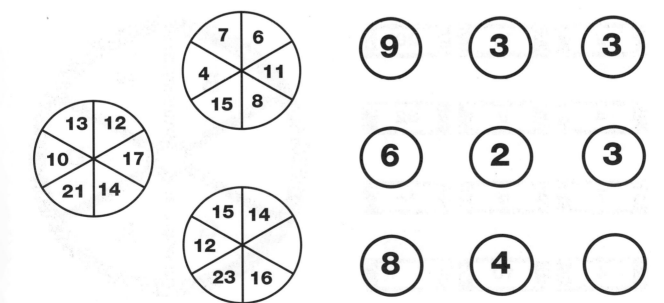

LEVEL

5

25 PUZZLE

Draw the correct symbols in the empty box.

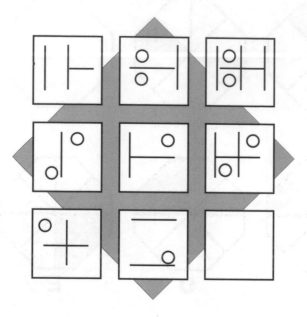

26 PUZZLE

Which number replaces the blank and completes the sequence?

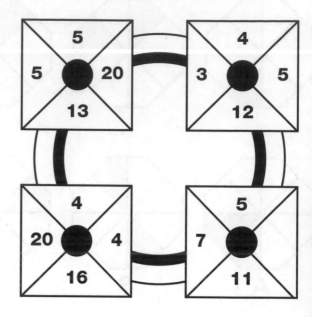

27 PUZZLE

Which number is missing from the empty box?

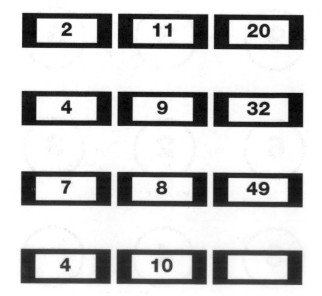

28 PUZZLE

Which letter should be entered into the empty segment?

Which letter replaces the blank and completes the sequence?

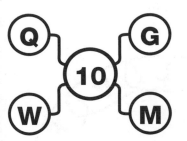 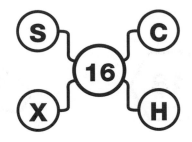 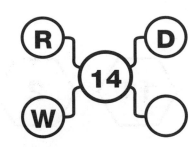

Which number goes in the empty segment?

Which number should be written in the empty circle?

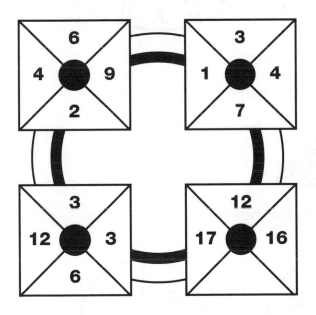 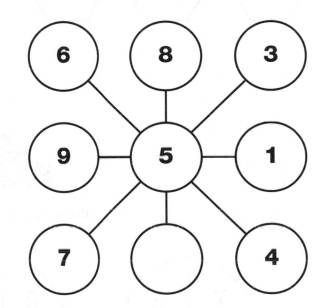

Which number completes the middle star?

LEVEL 5

Which number completes this puzzle?

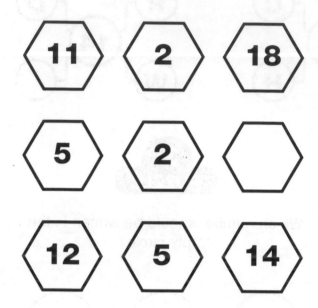

2 PUZZLE

Fill in the missing letter to complete the chain.

3 PUZZLE

Which number is missing?

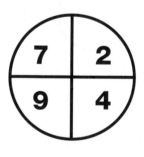

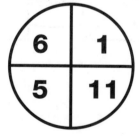

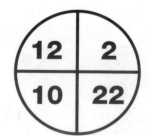

4 PUZZLE

Which number is missing from the empty segment?

5 PUZZLE

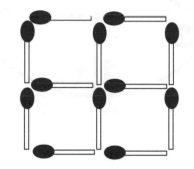

These 12 matches are arranged to give 4 equal areas. Can you rearrange the matches to give 6 equal areas, without adding, removing or breaking any matches?

6 PUZZLE

Which letter should be added to the empty segment?

7 PUZZLE

Which number finishes this grid?

5	7	6	8
10	4	6	6
5	7	10	4
12	4	4	

LEVEL

Which number is missing?

 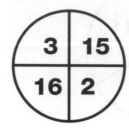

Which number is needed to complete the wheel?

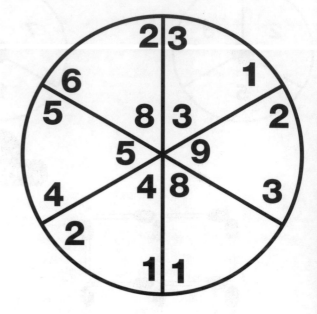

10 PUZZLE

Enter every number between 1 and 8 inclusive in this grid so that no two consecutive numbers are in adjacent squares.

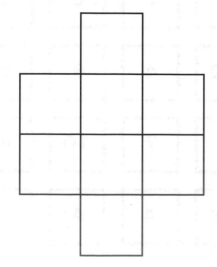

11 PUZZLE

Which letter replaces the blank and completes the sequence?

F	I
J	G
N	Q
R	O
V	Y
Z	

Which letter should be placed in the empty square?

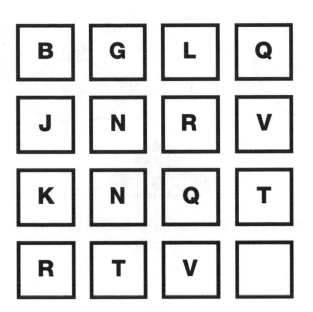

Which number is missing from this wheel?

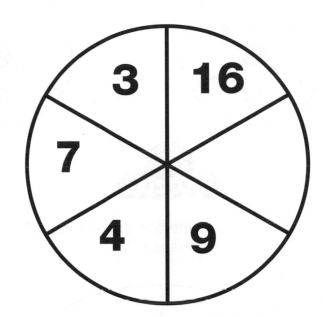

Enter the correct numbers in the blank segments and complete this puzzle.

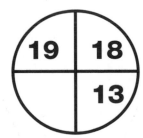
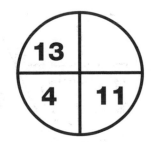

LEVEL

6

59

15 PUZZLE

Which number is needed to complete the third grid?

 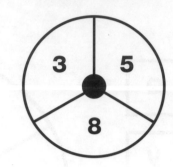 

16 PUZZLE

Which number is the odd one out in each shape?

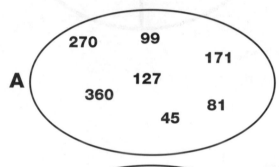

17 PUZZLE

Which number needs to added to the last oval?

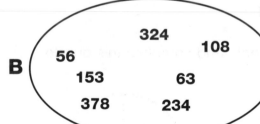

18 PUZZLE

Which number is missing from the last triangle?

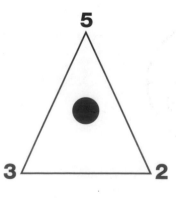 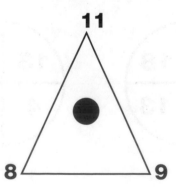 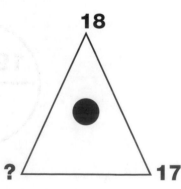

19 PUZZLE

Which letter replaces the blank and completes the sequence?

A	G	L
P	S	U

B	I	O
T	X	A

D	L	S
Y	D	

20 PUZZLE

Which number is missing?

1	3

3	4

4	7

7	11

11	18

18	

21 PUZZLE

Which character is needed to fill the blank segment?

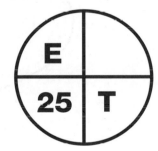

22 PUZZLE

Which number is missing from the last grid?

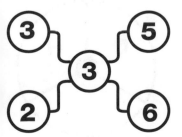
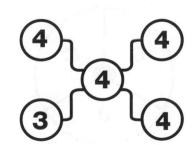
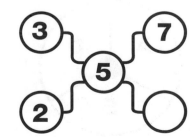

LEVEL

6

23 PUZZLE

Which number is missing from the final ellipse?

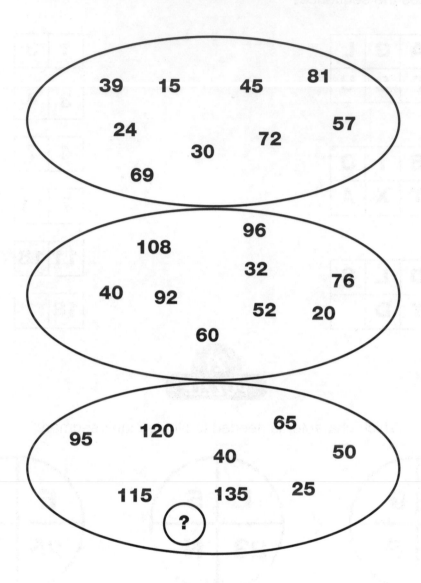

24 PUZZLE

Fill in the missing letter.

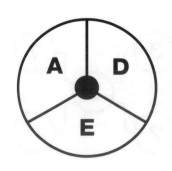
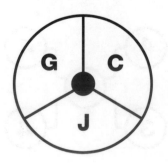
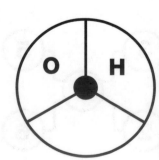

PUZZLE 25

Which letter is missing from the bottom circle?

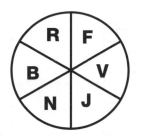

PUZZLE 26

What goes in the empty circle?

PUZZLE 27

Which number is missing from this wheel?

PUZZLE 28

Enter the missing number to complete this grid.

L
E
V
E
L

6

63

Which of the bottom grids logically goes in the centre of this puzzle?

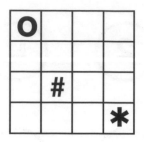
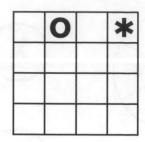

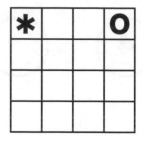
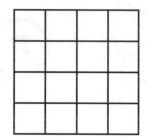
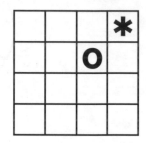

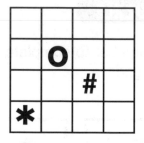
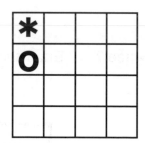
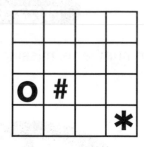

A

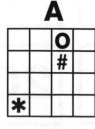

B

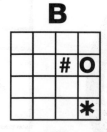

C

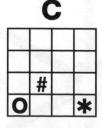

D

E

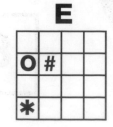

F

PUZZLE 1

Which number needs to be added to complete the last wheel?

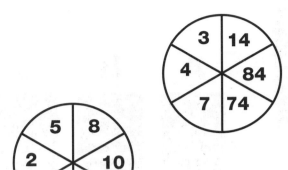

PUZZLE 2

Which number continues this sequence?

0

2

8

18

PUZZLE 3

Which letter goes in the empty link?

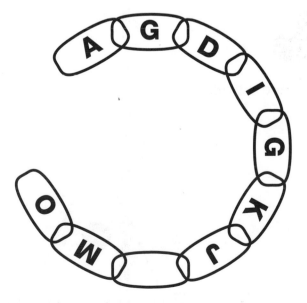

PUZZLE 4

Which number is missing?

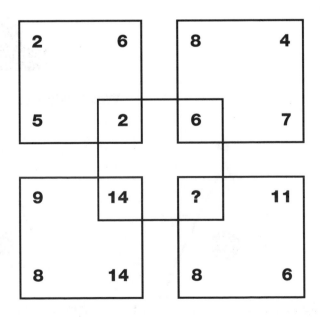

65

PUZZLE 5

Which domino will complete the third row?

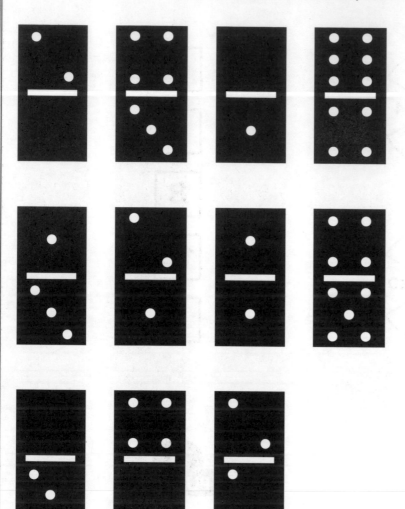

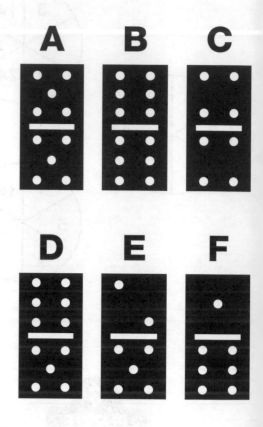

A B C

D E F

PUZZLE 6

Which letter tops the third triangle?

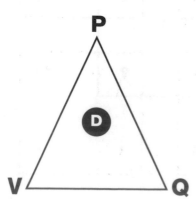

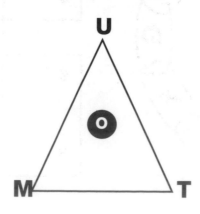

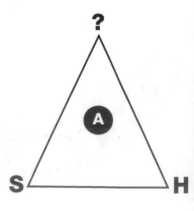

PUZZLE 7

Which number is missing from the grid?

6	2	5
10	3	16
18	6	60
34	15	

PUZZLE 8

Which number goes in the empty circle?

7   13   9

8   5   3

4   8   ( )

PUZZLE 9

Which number is needed to complete the puzzle?

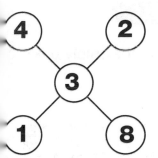 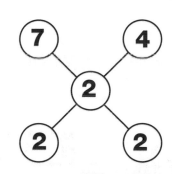 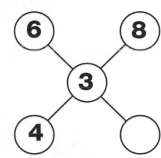

PUZZLE 10

Fill in the blank circle.

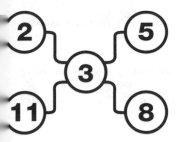  

LEVEL 7

PUZZLE 11

Which number completes this puzzle?

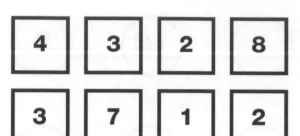

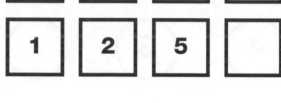

PUZZLE 12

Which number is missing?

PUZZLE 13

Which letter is the odd one out in each ellipse?

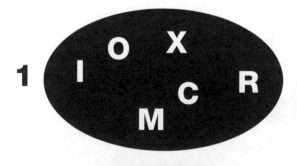
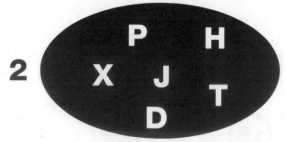

PUZZLE 14

Which number goes in the empty box?

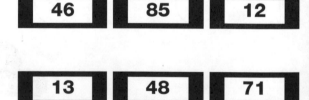

Which playing card is missing from this pattern?

LEVEL ⑦

PUZZLE 16

Which number needs to go in the blank segment?

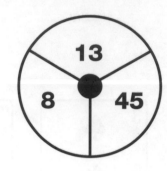

PUZZLE 17

Which number finishes the sequence?

PUZZLE 18

Which letter replaces the blank and completes the puzzle?

PUZZLE 19

Which letter needs to go in the blank circle?

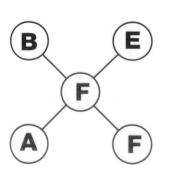

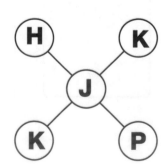

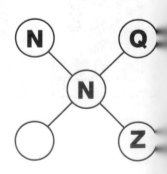

20 PUZZLE

Fill in the empty box with the correct letter.

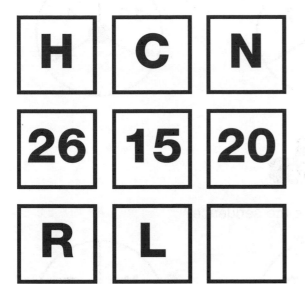

H	C	N
26	15	20
R	L	

21 PUZZLE

Which number is needed to finish this puzzle?

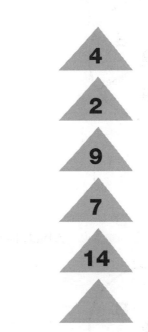

4
2
9
7
14

22 PUZZLE

Which letter goes in the empty circle?

B   F   H

O   G   V

Y   A

23 PUZZLE

Which number goes in the empty box and finishes the grid?

5	2	3
12	6	6

4	2	3
8	8	13

6	5	11
18	6	

PUZZLE 24

Which number goes in the blank segment?

PUZZLE 25

Which letter completes the sequence?

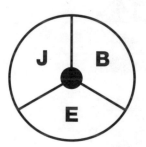

PUZZLE 26

Which number goes in the empty segment?

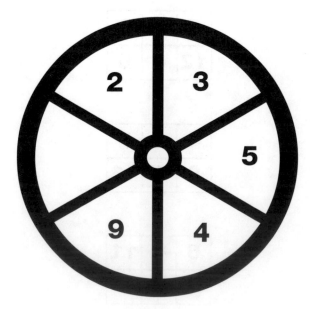

PUZZLE 27

Which number should be added to the empty circle?

28 PUZZLE

Which letter replaces the blank and completes the sequence?

B	Z	W	U
E	Q	O	R
G	J	L	P
F	H	K	

29 PUZZLE

Can you finish this sequence?

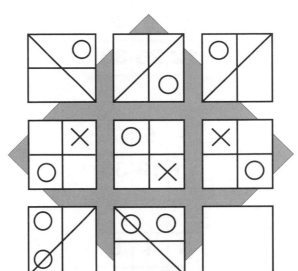

30 PUZZLE

What goes in the empty box?

W	B	4
C	U	9

N	L	5
S	F	1

Z	Q	7
T	I	

31 PUZZLE

Which letter is missing?

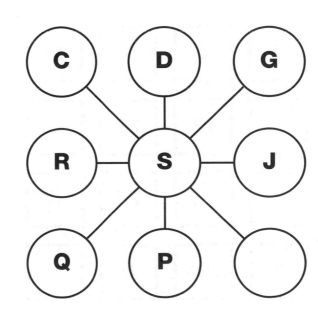

PUZZLE 1

Which number fits into the empty box?

5	6	8
12	20	36

4	5	7
11	19	35

3	4	6
10	18	

PUZZLE 2

Which letter replaces the blank and completes the sequence?

M	P	S

J	N	R

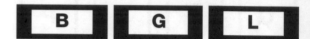

B	G	L

D	J	

PUZZLE 3

Which number would logically complete this grid?

9	3	4	11
5	17	18	3
3	16	21	8
4	9	6	

PUZZLE 4

What goes in the empty circle?

5	4	S
4	2	Z
2	3	

5
PUZZLE

Which piece fits back into the grid?

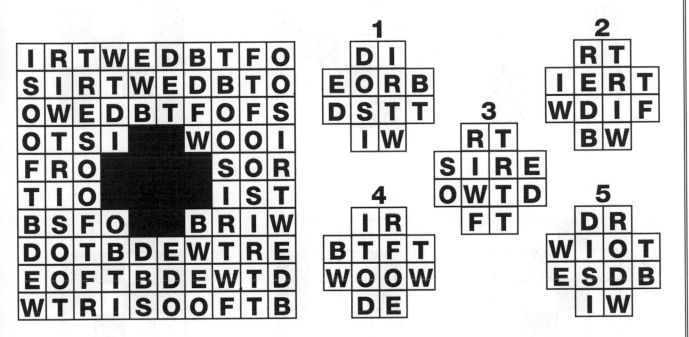

1
```
D I
E O R B
D S T T
  I W
```

2
```
R T
I E R T
W D I F
  B W
```

3
```
  R T
S I R E
O W T D
  F T
```

4
```
I R
B T F T
W O O W
  D E
```

5
```
  D R
W I O T
E S D B
    I W
```

Grid:
```
I R T W E D B T F O
S I R T W E D B T O
O W E D B T F O F S
O T S I ■ ■ W O O I
F R O ■ ■ ■ S O R
T I O ■ ■ I S T
B S F O ■ ■ B R I W
D O T B D E W T R E
E O F T B D E W T D
W T R I S O O F T B
```

6
PUZZLE

If two men stand back to back, walk in opposite directions for 4 metres, turn to the left and walk another 3 metres, what is the distance between them when they stop?

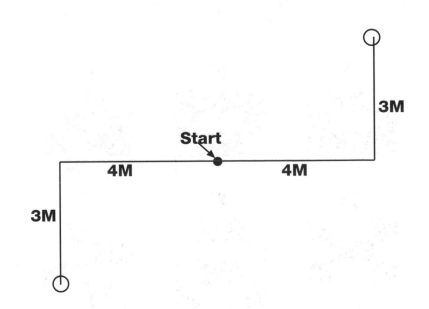

3M

Start

4M   4M

3M

PUZZLE 7

Which of the bottom squares fits logically at the end of this puzzle?

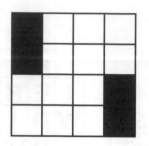
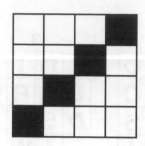

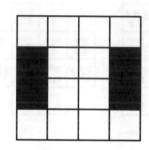

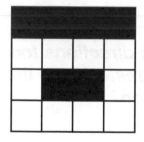

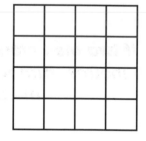

A   **B**   **C**

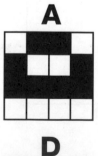
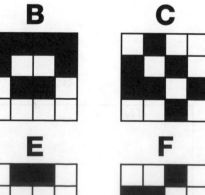

D   **E**   **F**

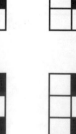

PUZZLE 8

Which number is missing from this sequence?

1	3

2	4

2	6

3	5

4	12

4	

PUZZLE 9

Which number replaces the question mark and completes the puzzle?

3	11		6	9
5	13	8		11

7	15	?		13
9	17		12	15

PUZZLE 10

Which two characters go into the empty boxes at the bottom of the table?

3	B

5	C

7	E

11	G

13	K

PUZZLE 11

Joan is extremely fussy about everything, particularly her numbers. She likes 225, but not 224. She prefers 900 to 800, and she absolutely loves 144, but loathes 145.

From this information can you tell if she would like 1600 or 1700?

PUZZLE 12

Luke challenged his twin sister Lucy to remove 8 matches to leave 2 squares whose edges do not touch, can you see how she managed it?

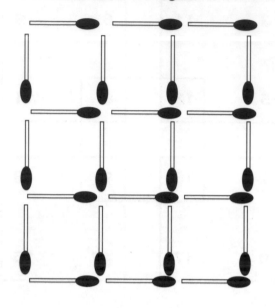

PUZZLE 13

Which number is missing from this puzzle?

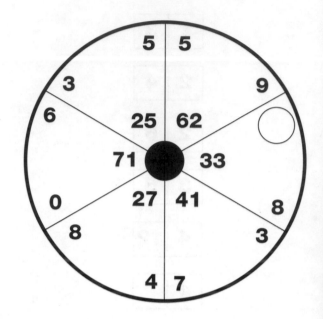

PUZZLE 14

Which number continues the sequence?

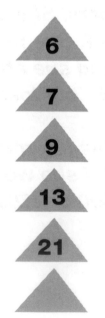

PUZZLE 15

Which number replaces the question mark and completes the sequence?

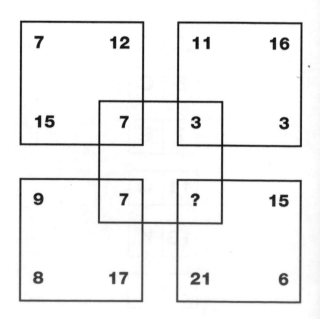

Simon showed Jason an arrangement of 9 matches which made 4 identical triangles. Jason then showed Simon how to use only 6 matches to produce the same 4 identical triangles. How is this possible?

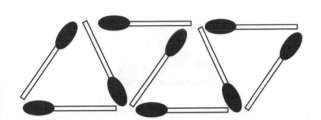

Which number is missing?

Which letter replaces the blank and completes the sequence?

Complete this puzzle by drawing what you think should appear in the empty box.

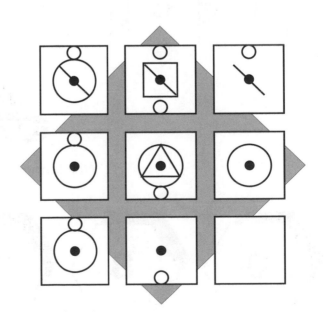

L E V E L

8

79

PUZZLE 20

Which number is missing from the middle of the last triangle?

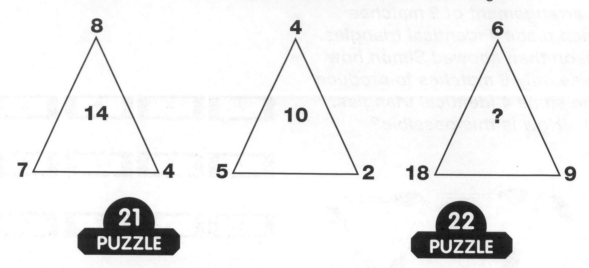

PUZZLE 21

Which number replaces the blank and completes the sequence?

PUZZLE 22

Which number is missing from the empty circle?

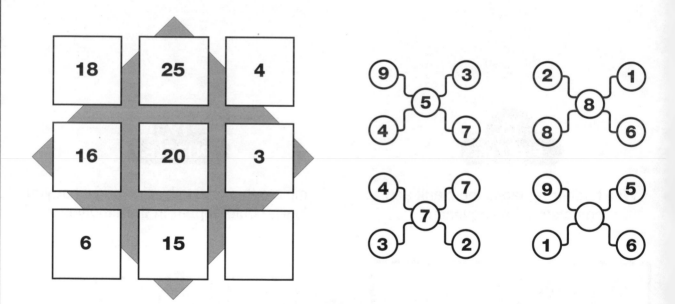

PUZZLE 23

Which number follows next?

Which box is the odd one out?

A

B

C

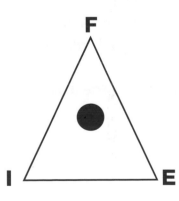

D

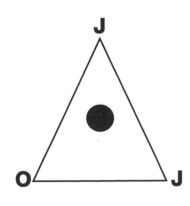

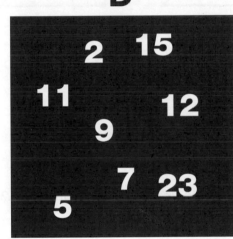

Which letter is missing?

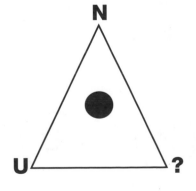

PUZZLE 26

Which letter goes in the empty segment to complete the sequence?

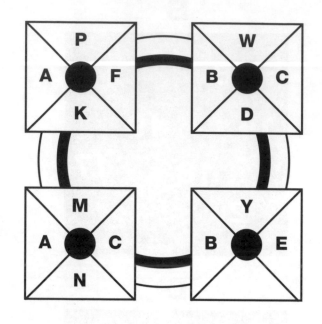

PUZZLE 27

Which number should go in the empty box?

4	7
2	2
6	9
8	12
3	1
7	

PUZZLE 28

Which letter goes in the empty circle?

PUZZLE 29

Melinda and her father love puzzles. When Melinda's cousin asked her how old she was she told her:

"If I doubled my age and subtracted 1, it would be the same as my father's age – and if you reverse the digits of his age, you get my age."

Can you work out their ages?

PUZZLE 30

Which number goes in the empty segment?

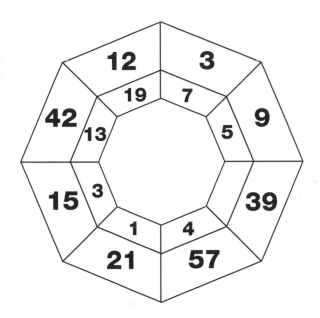

PUZZLE 31

Which number goes in the empty box?

PUZZLE 32

Which letter is missing from the bottom triangle?

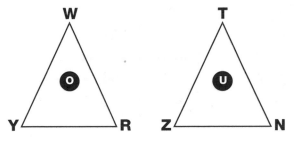

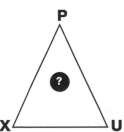

PUZZLE 33

Which number is missing from the last row?

Which number is missing from the centre of the last star?

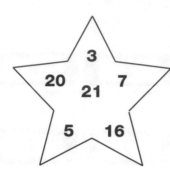

Which number comes next in this sequence?

9 - 7 - 8 - 6 - 7 - 5 - 6 - ?

3
PUZZLE

Which letter is missing from the blank segment?

PUZZLE 4

Which number completes this puzzle?

PUZZLE 5

Which number is missing from the last wheel?

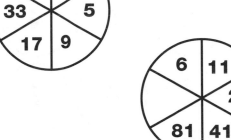

PUZZLE 6

Fill in the blank point of the third star.

PUZZLE 7

Which number is missing from the last triangle?

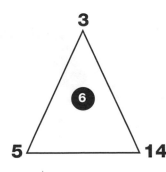

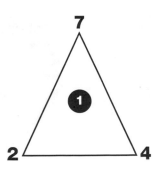

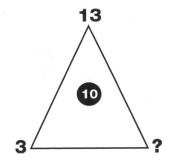

LEVEL ●●●●●●●●⑨○○○○○○○○○○

85

8
PUZZLE

Which number goes in the middle of the grid?

6   4   2

2   8   6   1   3

9   3   4   ☐   6   6   1

4   7   6   3   2

2   1   1

2   3   4   5   6   7   8   9

9
PUZZLE

Which number is missing?

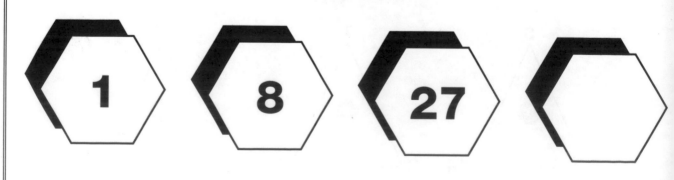

1   8   27   ☐

PUZZLE 10

Which letter replaces the blank and completes the sequence?

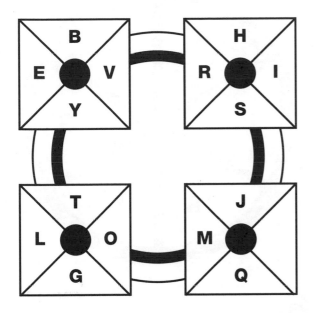

PUZZLE 11

Which number logically completes the grid?

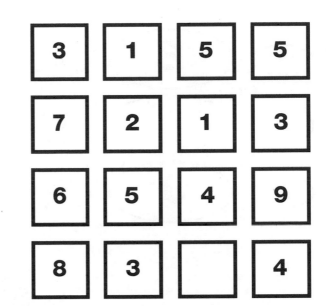

PUZZLE 12

Which letter is missing from around the centre of the wheel?

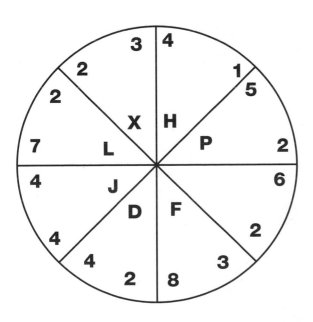

PUZZLE 13

Which letter goes in the empty box?

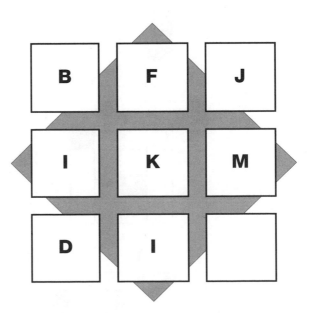

14 PUZZLE

Which letter goes in the centre?

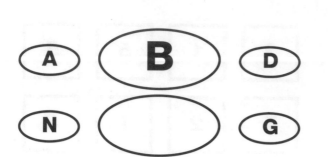

15 PUZZLE

Which number is missing from the wheel?

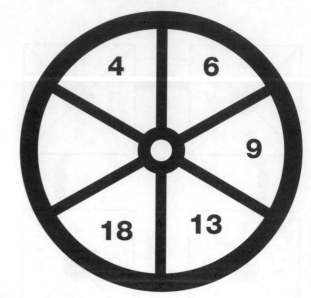

16 PUZZLE

Which of the bottom boxes completes the sequence?

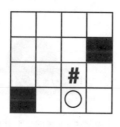 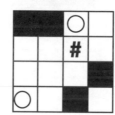 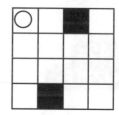

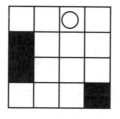 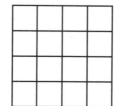 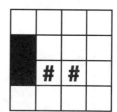

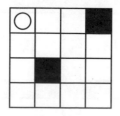 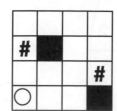 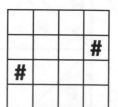

A   **B**   **C**   **D**

 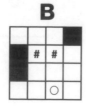 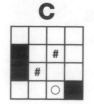 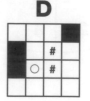

9

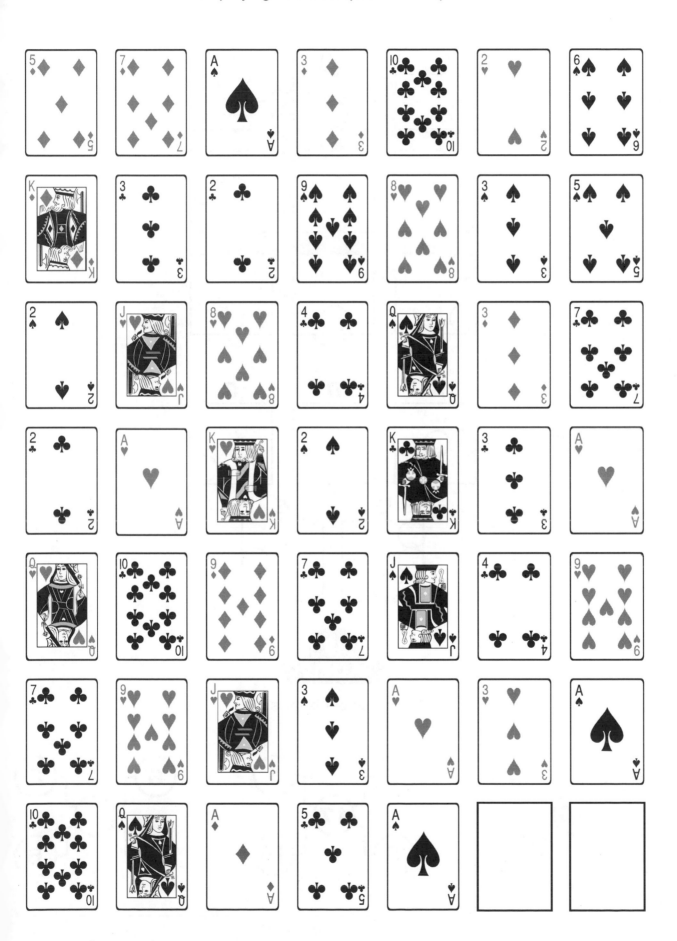

PUZZLE 17

Which playing cards complete the sequence?

Which of the bottom boxes completes this sequence?

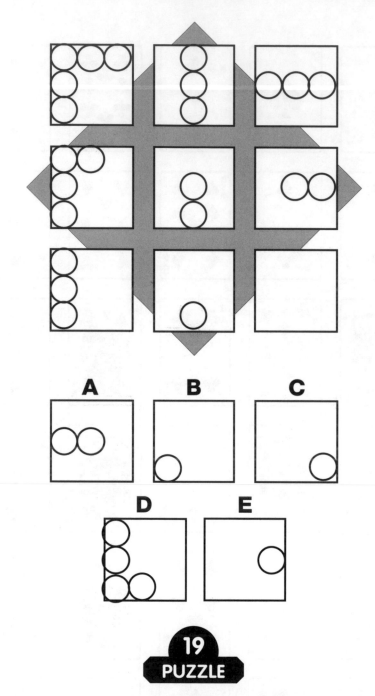

A   B   C

D   E

Which number is missing?

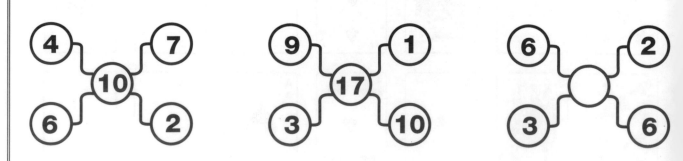

20 PUZZLE

Which letter replaces the blank and completes the puzzle?

A　C　F

J　L　O

S　U　◯

21 PUZZLE

Find the missing value.

24	63	24	21	
@	@	@	!	33
!	Σ	!	Ω	?
Ω	Σ	Ω	Ω	33
!	!	!	@	27

22 PUZZLE

Using these six matches, make three squares all the same size.

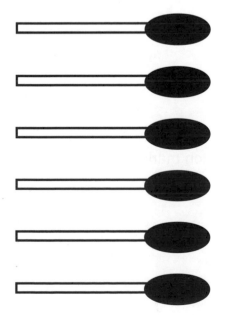

23 PUZZLE

Which number is missing from the empty segment?

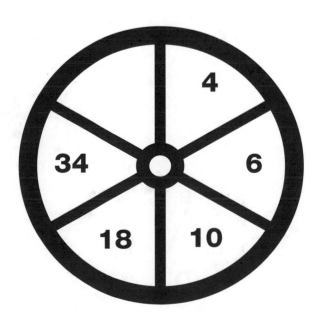

24 PUZZLE

Which number is missing?

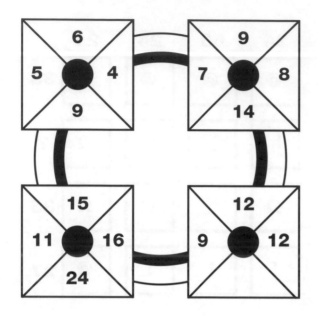

25 PUZZLE

Becky had a large packet of biscuits. After eating the first one she gave half of what she had left to her friend Ella. After eating another one, she gave half of what was left to Chelsea, leaving her with just 5 biscuits.

How many biscuits were in the packet to start with?

26 PUZZLE

Which letter is missing from the last star?

27 PUZZLE

Which letter replaces the question mark?

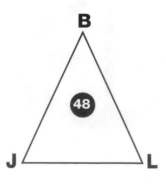

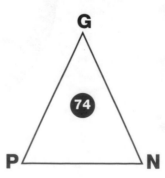

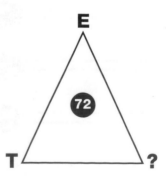

Which letter goes in the empty circle?

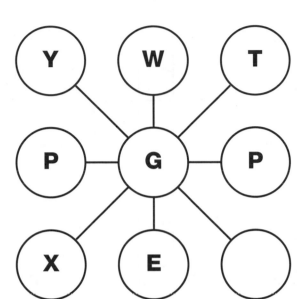

Which letter goes in the empty box at the bottom of the pile?

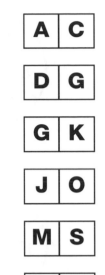

Which number is missing from the empty segment?

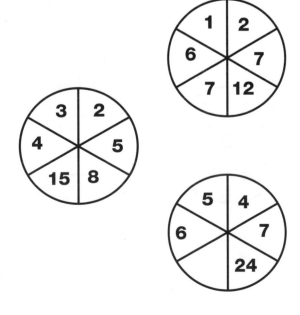

Which number comes next to continue this sequence?

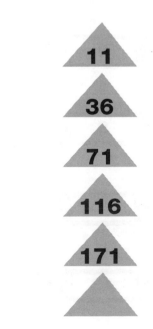

LEVEL

93

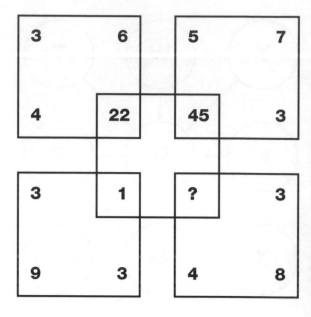

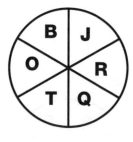

L E V E L

10

94

PUZZLE 5

Which letter is missing from the empty segment in the bottom circle?

PUZZLE 6

Which number replaces the question mark?

PUZZLE 7

Which number goes in the blank box and completes the puzzle?

PUZZLE 8

Which letter goes in the empty segment?

9 PUZZLE

Which letter finishes the third circle?

  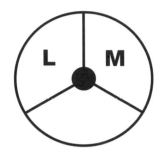

10 PUZZLE

Which number is missing from the last grid??

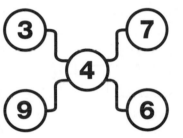 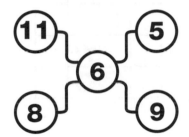 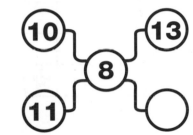

11 PUZZLE

Which number replaces the question mark?

12 PUZZLE

Complete this puzzle.

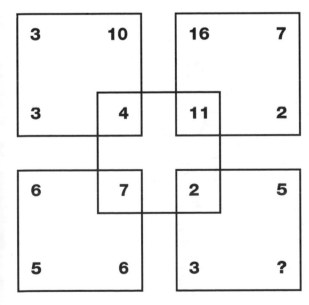

L
E
V
E
L

10

95

Which of the bottom boxes completes this sequence?

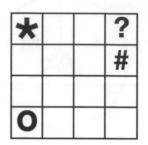
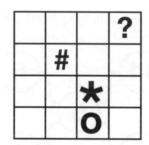
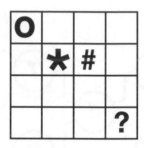

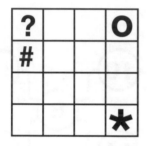
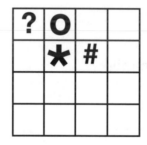
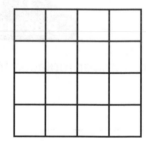

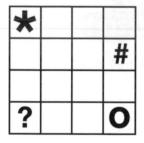
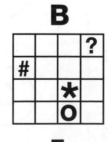
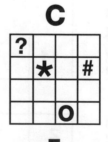

A   **B**   **C**

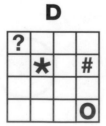
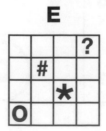
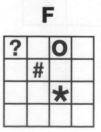

D   **E**   **F**

14 PUZZLE

Which letter finishes the third circle?

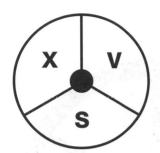

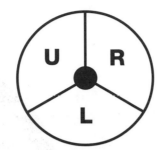

15 PUZZLE

Which number completes the last grid?

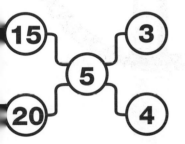

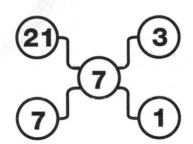

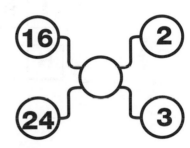

16 PUZZLE

Which number goes in the empty box?

17 PUZZLE

Which letter completes this puzzle?

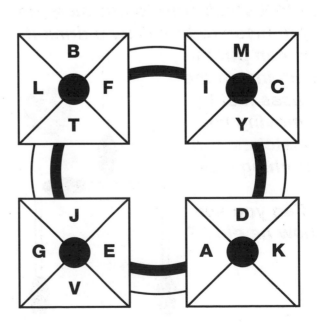

LEVEL

10

PUZZLE 18

Which letter goes in the empty box?

C	L
H	Q
F	O
K	T
I	R
N	

PUZZLE 19

Which letter completes the wheel?

PUZZLE 20

John arranges 4 matches to make an upside down glass and puts a small coin to one side. He promises to buy Gary a drink if he can put the coin inside the glass just by moving two matches and nothing else.

Can you see how he did it?

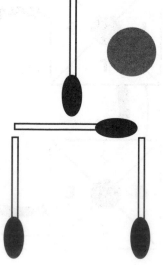

PUZZLE 21

Which number comes next in this sequence?

7

13

24

45

Which number is missing from the last grid?

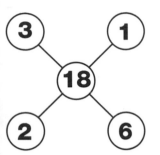
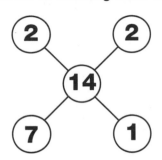
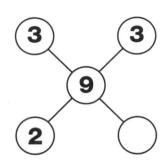

Which number is missing?

Fill in the empty ellipse.

What shape will replace the question mark?

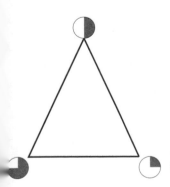
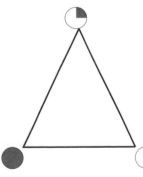
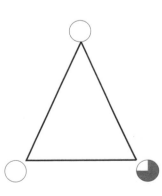
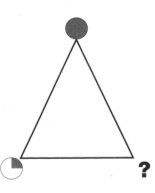

?

LEVEL

10

99

26 PUZZLE

Which letter goes in the empty link and completes the chain?

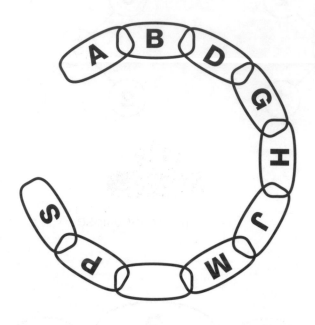

27 PUZZLE

Which number is missing from the middle of the last grid?

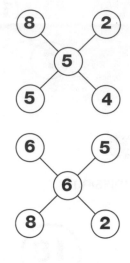
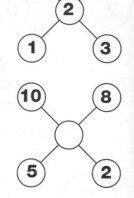

28 PUZZLE

Which number continues the sequence?

8

10

16

34

29 PUZZLE

Draw the correct markings in the last box.

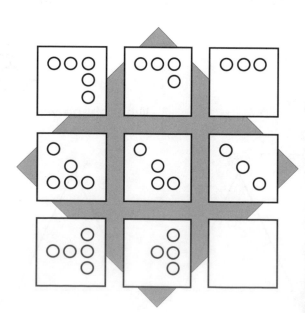

Which shape is the odd one out and why?

10

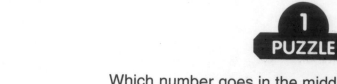

PUZZLE 1

Which number goes in the middle of the third triangle?

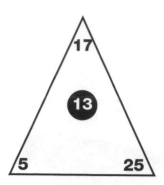

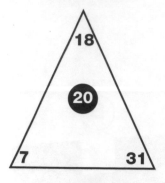

PUZZLE 2

Move one match and make this sum correct.

PUZZLE 3

Which number goes in the empty box and completes the puzzle?

3	6	3
10	3	7
8	1	

PUZZLE 4

Which number is missing from the bottom grid?

9	4	6
0	4	3

7	1	3
0	3	1

5	0	4
0	2	

PUZZLE 5

Which number completes the grid?

PUZZLE 6

Move just four matches to make seven squares.

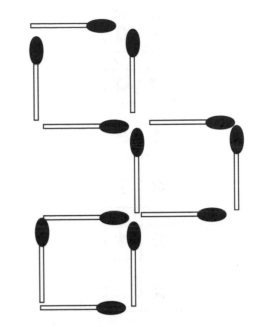

PUZZLE 7

Which number replaces the question mark?

2	4	5	6
3	2	7	7
11	10	8	8
15	?	11	12

PUZZLE 8

Which letter goes in the bottom box?

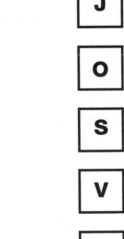

J

O

S

V

LEVEL

PUZZLE 9

What is missing from the empty box?

1	0
J	Q
1	8
R	I
2	4
X	

PUZZLE 10

Which number continues the sequence?

1
5
13
29

PUZZLE 11

What time should the blank watch be showing?

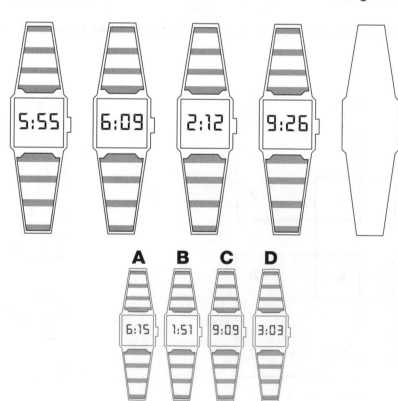

104

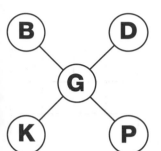

PUZZLE 12

Which letter should go in the empty circle?

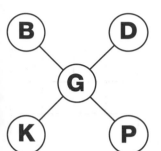

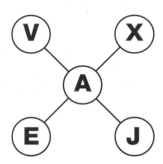

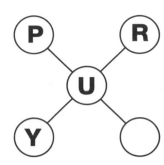

PUZZLE 13

Which number should replace the question mark?

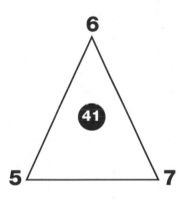

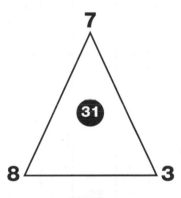

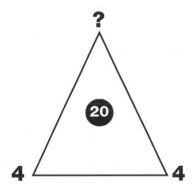

PUZZLE 14

Which of these numbered pieces will fit in the centre of the grid?

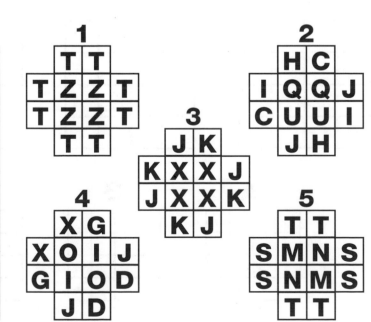

5	3	7	9	1	1	9	7	3	5
3	4	2	7	8	8	7	2	4	3
7	2	5	1	2	2	1	5	2	7
9	0	1	6			6	1	0	9
1	8	2				2	8	1	
1	8	2				2	8	1	
9	0	1	6			6	1	0	9
7	2	5	1	2	2	1	5	2	7
3	4	2	7	8	8	7	2	4	3
5	3	7	9	1	1	9	7	3	5

1

	T	T	
T	Z	Z	T
T	Z	Z	T
	T	T	

2

	H	C	
I	Q	Q	J
C	U	U	I
	J	H	

3

	J	K	
K	X	X	J
J	X	X	K
	K	J	

4

	X	G	
X	O	I	J
G	I	O	D
	J	D	

5

	T	T	
S	M	N	S
S	N	M	S
	T	T	

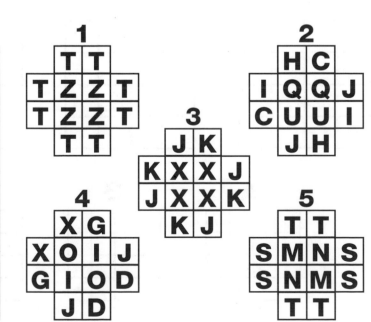

105

PUZZLE 15

Which of the bottom boxes finishes this puzzle?

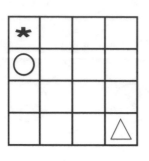 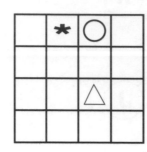 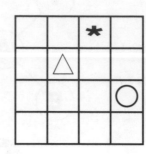 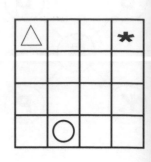

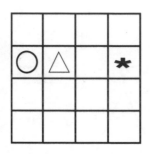 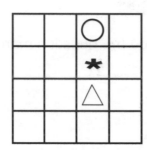 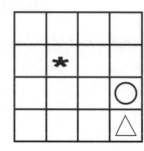 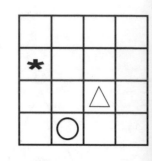

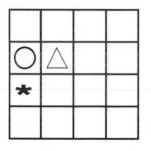 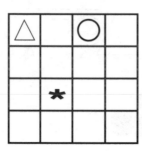 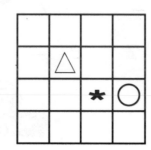 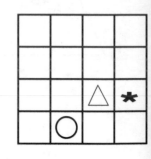

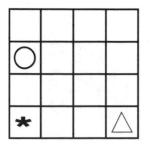 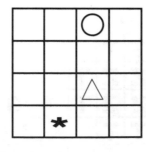 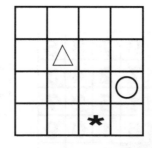 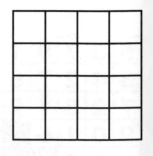

A   **B**   **C**   **D**

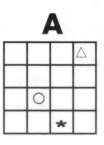 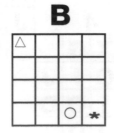 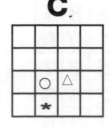 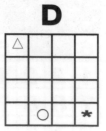

What time should be showing next?

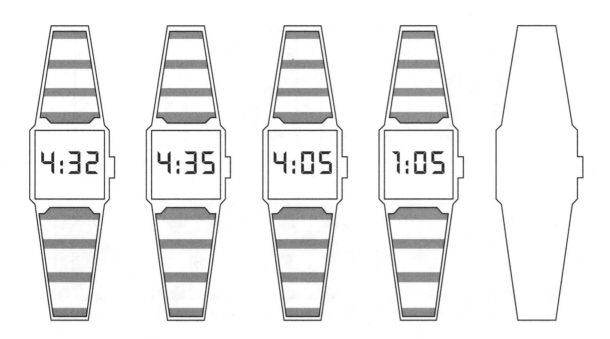

Which letter goes in the empty corner?

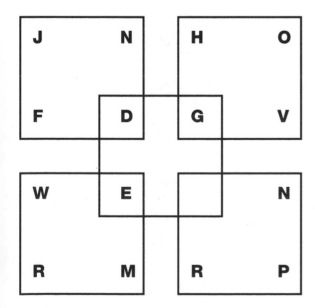

Each number from 1-25 inclusive is to be put in the grid so that each row, column and corner to corner line adds up to 65.

21				1
	8			
		13		
				16
25			2	

LEVEL

19 PUZZLE

Which of the bottom playing cards completes the top line?

     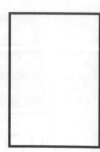

20 PUZZLE

Which number is missing from the empty segment in the web?

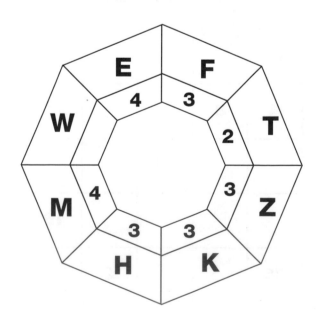

21 PUZZLE

Which number is needed to complete the puzzle?

PUZZLE

Which playing card completes the puzzle?

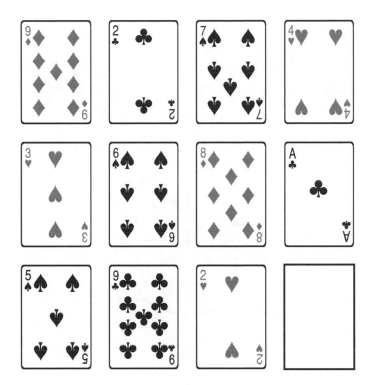

PUZZLE

Fill in the empty box.

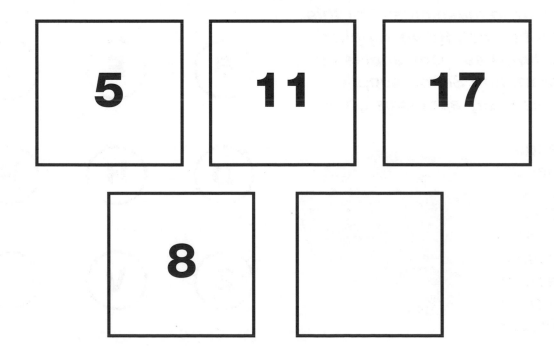

 L E V E L

110

24
PUZZLE

Which number is missing from the bottom circle?

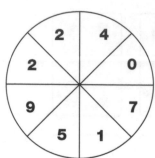

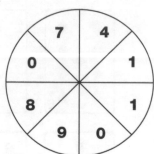

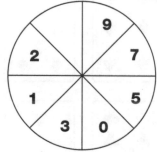

25
PUZZLE

Simon, Steve and Stewart are all apple farmers who pool their crop each year to make cider. For this year's harvest, Steve supplied three times as many apples as Stewart, and Simon supplied twice as many apples as Steve.

If the total number of apples supplied is 900 tonnes, how many did each of them contribute?

26
PUZZLE

Which letter is missing from the empty circle?

 H N

Z V

Edward spent £21 on drinks for a party. If the bottle of vodka he purchased was twice the price of the case of beer, and the lemonade was half the price of the beer, how much did Edward spend on the beer?

Which number replaces the blank?

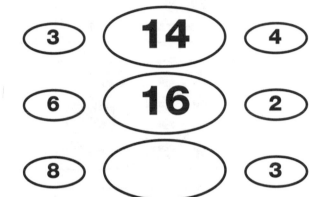

Which numbers are missing from this puzzle?

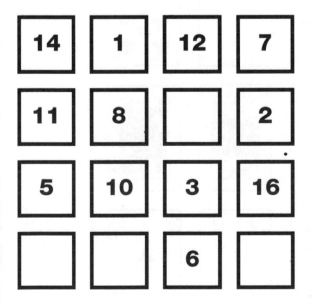

Move two matches to make seven squares.

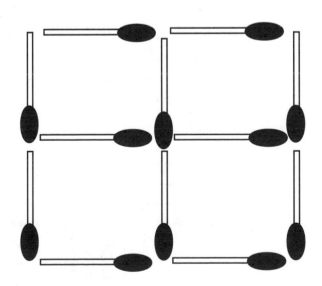

LEVEL

11

Which two playing cards are needed to complete this puzzle?

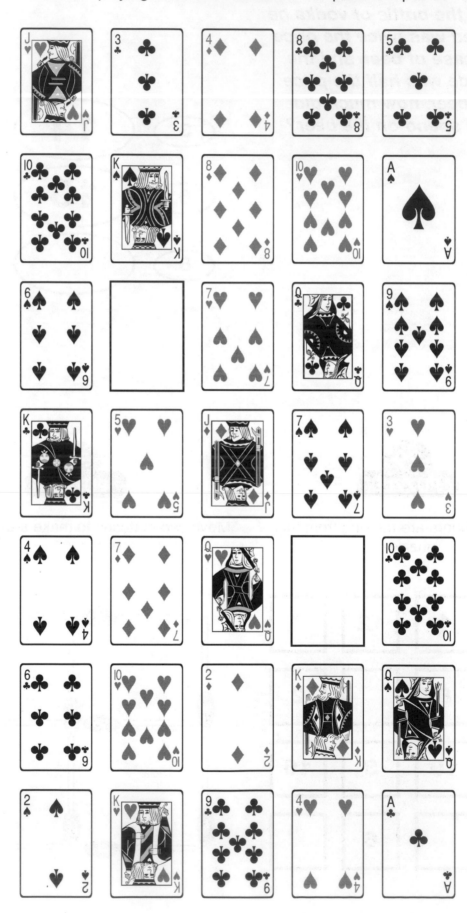

PUZZLE 2

Rearrange these coins into a five-line shape, with each line containing 4 coins.

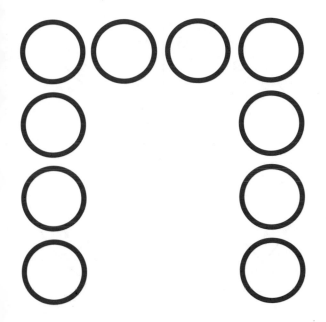

PUZZLE 3

Which number goes in the empty shape?

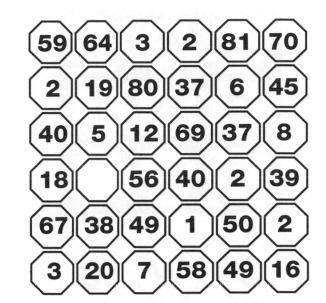

PUZZLE 4

Which number is the odd one out in each ellipse?

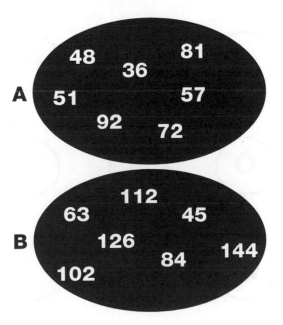

PUZZLE 5

Which number is missing?

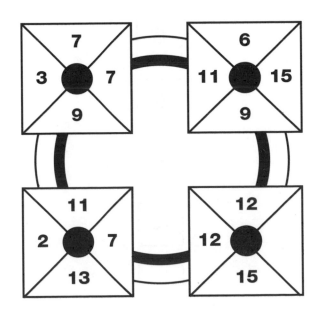

LEVEL 12

113

Which of the three letters at the bottom completes the puzzle?

Which number is missing?

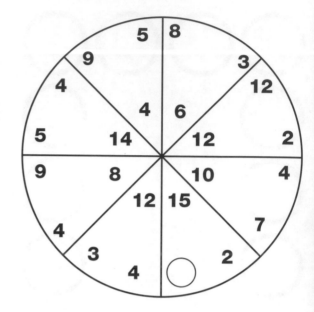

8 PUZZLE

Which number continues the sequence?

3

5

9

15

9 PUZZLE

Which letter replaces the blank and completes the sequence?

Which playing cards are needed to fill in the blanks?

11 PUZZLE

Which number goes in the empty box?

10	5	6
1	12	8
7	9	5
17	1	

12 PUZZLE

What is the missing line value?

35	47	38	24	
⊙	▲	▲	▲	?
#	⊙	⊙	#	40
#	*	#	#	21
*	*	*	*	48

13 PUZZLE

Which letter goes in the middle?

F

D S G

C R B T H

B Q Z ( ) C V J

P Y D W K

N X L

M

A B C D E F G H

PUZZLE 14

Which number comes next?

1 - 2 - 5 - 10 - 13 - 26 - 29 - ?

PUZZLE 15

Which number goes in the middle of the last star?

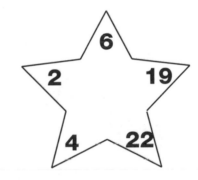

PUZZLE 16

Complete the puzzle.

PUZZLE 17

What is the missing line value?

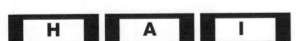

E	L	Q
H	A	I
D	O	S
S	F	

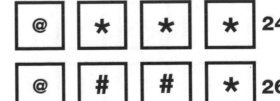

36	23	24	?	
@	*	#	▲	27
@	▲	▲	#	29
@	*	*	*	24
@	#	#	*	26

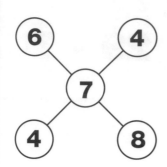

18 PUZZLE

Fill in the empty circle.

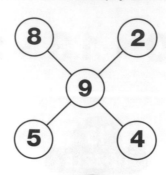

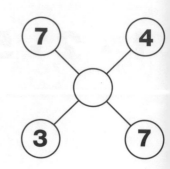

19 PUZZLE

Which letter goes in the empty circle?

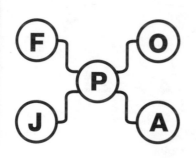

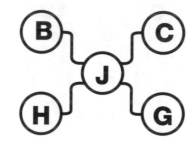

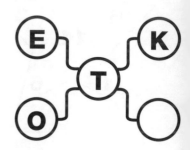

20 PUZZLE

What is the missing line value?

21 PUZZLE

What goes in the blank corner of the middle square?

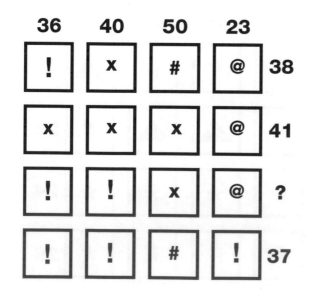

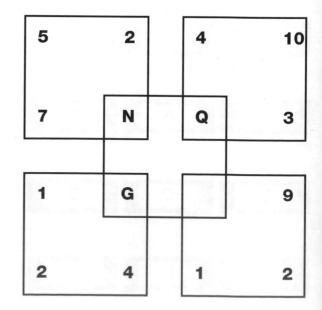

PUZZLE 22

Which number is missing from this column of boxes?

3	1
2	5
8	4
7	12
17	
16	23

PUZZLE 23

Helen's watch needs repairing. She sets it correctly at 4:12pm but three hours later it shows 8:00pm. After a further two hours she notices that it reads 10:32pm.

She goes to bed early and gets up when her watch shows 6:46am.

What time is it really?

PUZZLE 24

What is missing from the blank segment?

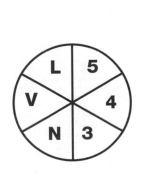

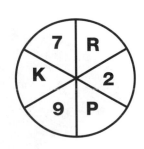

PUZZLE 25

Which number is needed to finish the puzzle correctly?

2	5	3	7
9	8	2	1
4	8	0	8
5	3	4	

PUZZLE 26

Which number needs to be added to the last grid?

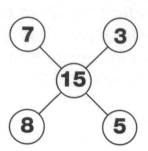

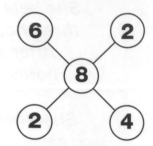

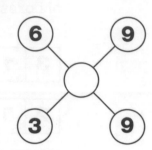

PUZZLE 27

Which number goes in the blank segment?

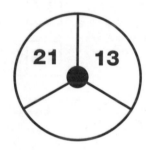

PUZZLE 28

Which number completes the puzzle?

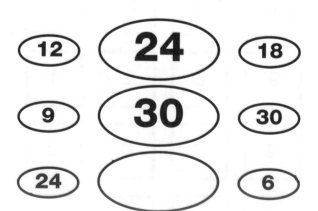

PUZZLE 29

Which number replaces the question mark?

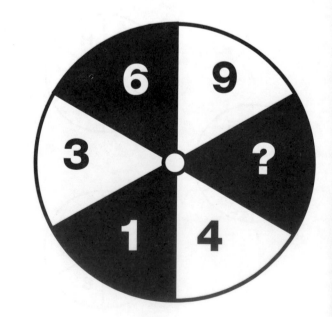

Which of the bottom boxes goes in the middle of this sequence?

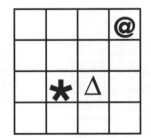

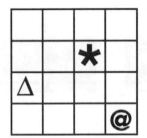

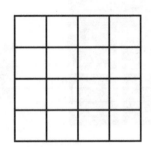

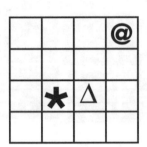

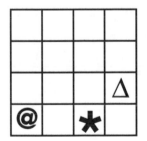

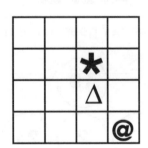

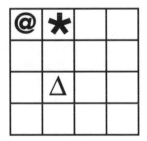

A

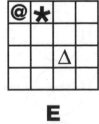

B

C

D

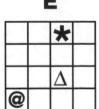

E

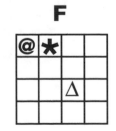

F

PUZZLE 2

Which domino fits into the empty space in this arrangement?

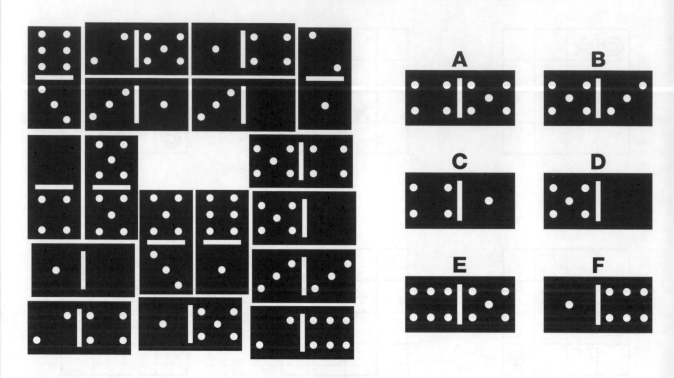

PUZZLE 3

Which number goes in the middle?

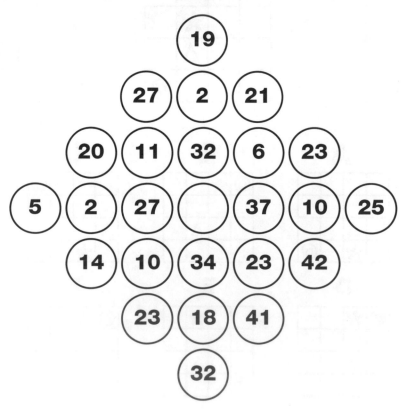

PUZZLE 4

Which number is missing from the web?

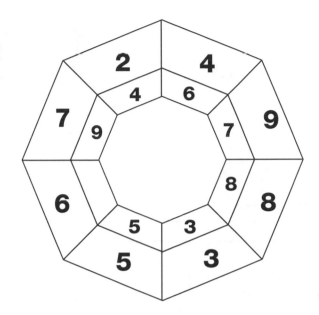

PUZZLE 5

Which number is missing from the wheel?

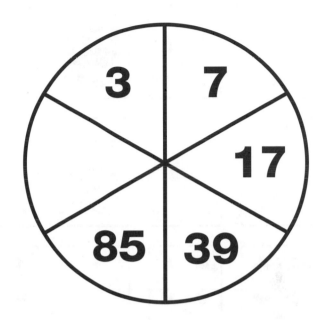

PUZZLE 6

Which watch is the odd one out?

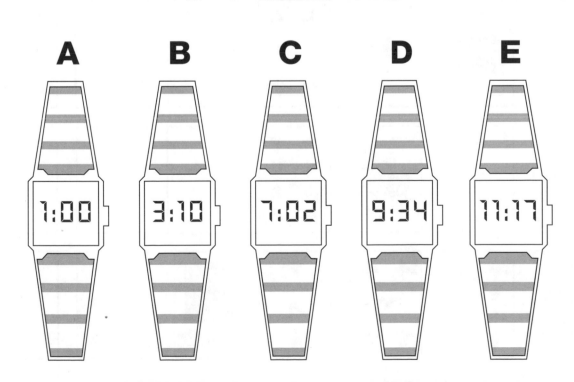

PUZZLE

Which playing cards are needed to fill in the blanks?

PUZZLE 8

Which number completes the third triangle?

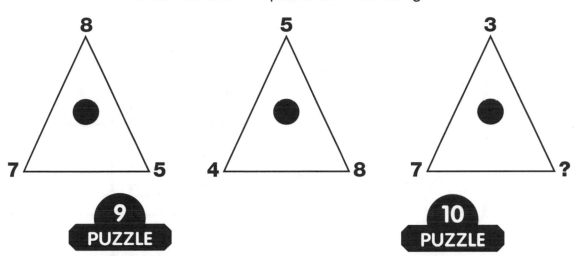

8
7 ● 5

5
4 ● 8

3
7 ● ?

PUZZLE 9

What time should the blank clock show?

PUZZLE 10

What is missing from the empty segment?

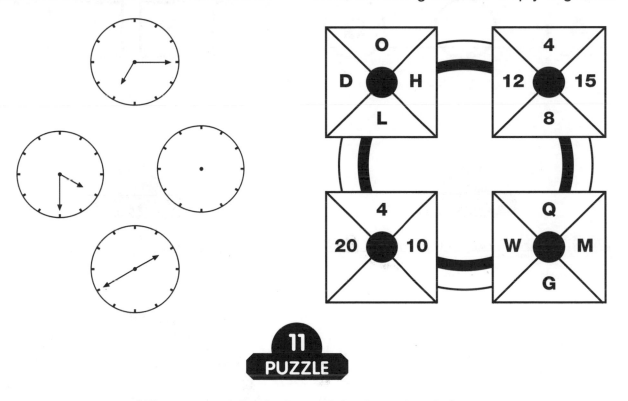

O
D ● H
L

4
12 ● 15
8

4
20 ● 10

Q
W ● M
G

PUZZLE 11

What goes at the bottom of the last triangle?

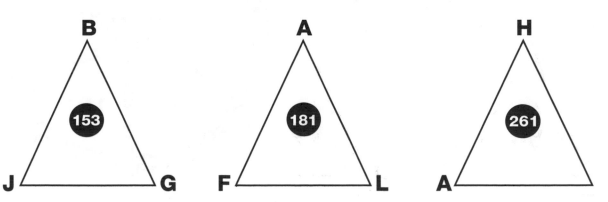

B
153
J   G

A
181
F   L

H
261
A

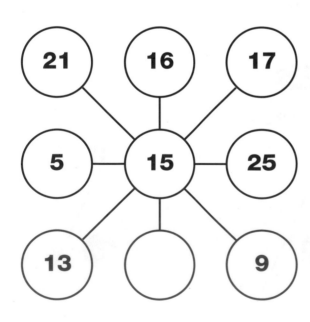

LEVEL

PUZZLE 12

Which letter replaces the blank and completes the sequence?

I L O

R U X

A ☐ G

PUZZLE 13

Which letters finish the grid?

H	X	J	Z
U	O	D	H
	G	V	P
I	Y	I	

PUZZLE 14

Which number goes in the empty circle?

21 16 17

5 15 25

13 ☐ 9

PUZZLE 15

Which letter completes the wheel?

F I

O ☐

R U

126

PUZZLE 16

Which two letters are missing from the bottom grids?

PUZZLE 17

Fill in the correct number.

3	5	8	7
10	2	7	13
6	6	14	22
9	2	5	

PUZZLE 18

Fill in the empty segment.

PUZZLE 19

Which number is missing from the last circle?

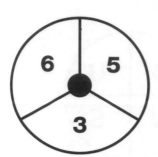  

PUZZLE 20

Which number goes at the top of the third star?

PUZZLE 21

Which letter logically goes in the blank segment?

PUZZLE 22

Complete the bottom grid.

3	8	18
5	10	20

4	10	22
6	12	24

7	16	
9	18	

PUZZLE 23

Which number is needed to complete this puzzle?

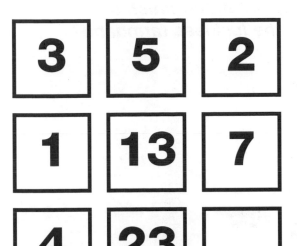

PUZZLE 24

Finish the chain by filling in the blank link.

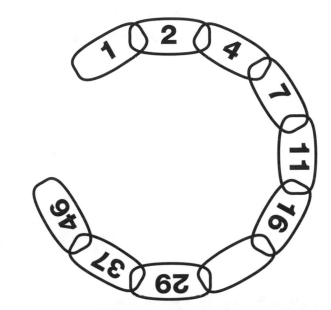

PUZZLE 25

Which letter goes at the bottom?

PUZZLE 26

Which number goes in the empty box?

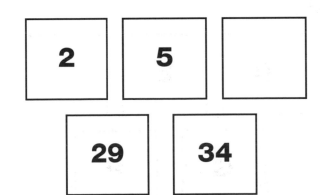

Farmer Giles has sent his livestock to market for sale but the farmhand has forgotten how much he was to sell each animal for. The farmer though had drawn him some pictures which showed the equivalent value of each of the animals but didn't finish it.
Can you solve the problem for the luckless farmhand?

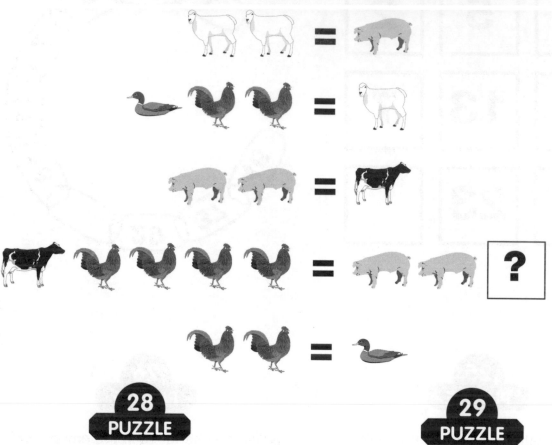

L E V E L

13

130

28 PUZZLE

Which letter goes in the empty square and completes the puzzle?

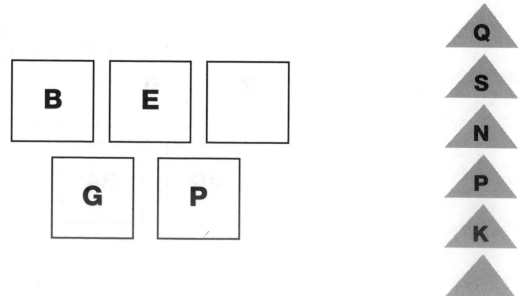

29 PUZZLE

Which letter replaces the blank and completes the sequence?

Q

S

N

P

K

Which letter is missing from the chain?

Which number is needed to complete the puzzle?

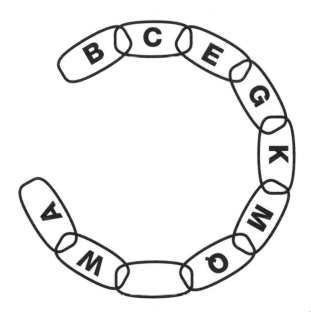

5	7	10
25	19	
32	40	49

Roy, Molly, Frank and Maude are all keen gardeners. As the diagrams show, they each have room for 10 plants in their plots so they can grow either flowers, trees or vegetables.

Ray grows more flowers than Maude, and Molly has more trees in her garden than Frank. Together Maude and Molly have more vegetables than the men.

Which garden belongs to each gardener?

1

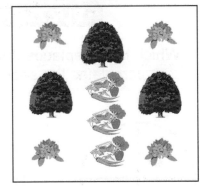

2

3

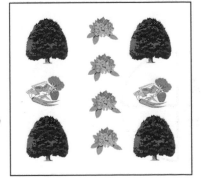

4

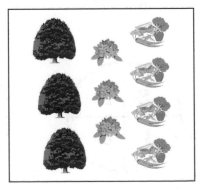

LEVEL

14

PUZZLE 4

Here is a 4 x 3 grid with twelve matches defining a triangle which takes up half of the area. Move just 4 matches to reduce the area by a half.

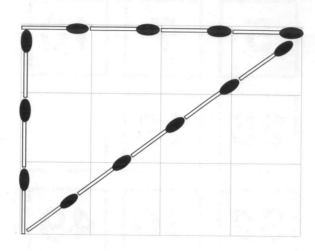

PUZZLE 5

Using the digits 0-5 inclusive, write one number in each small circle so that the values around each large circle add up to ten.

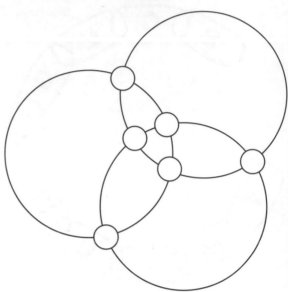

PUZZLE 6

Which letter replaces the blank and completes the sequence?

PUZZLE 7

Which letter goes at the bottom of the column?

A

E

F

H

PUZZLE 8

Which number is missing from the last circle?

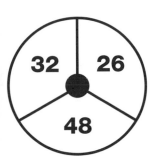 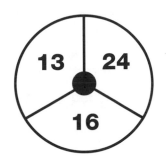 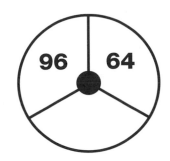

PUZZLE 9

Which playing card completes this puzzle?

LEVEL

14

10 PUZZLE

Which watch goes in the blank space?

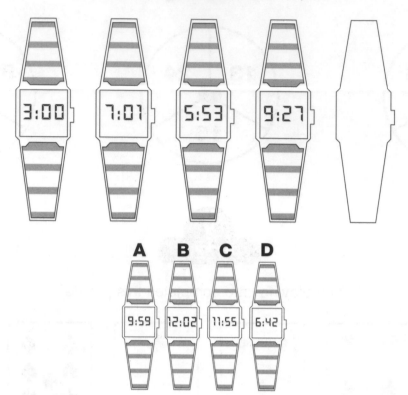

3:00   7:01   5:53   9:27

A 9:59   **B** 12:02   **C** 11:55   **D** 6:42

11 PUZZLE

Which number is missing?

| 1 |
| 5 |
| 9 |
| 15 |
| |

12 PUZZLE

Complete this puzzle.

48   **7**   21

531   **5**   72

54   ( )   51

Which playing card finishes the puzzle?

Which letter replaces the blank and completes the sequence?

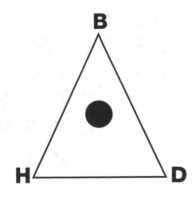

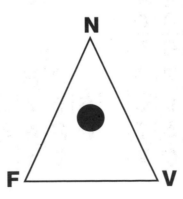

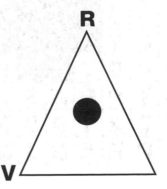

15 PUZZLE

Which letter replaces the blank and completes the sequence?

J M P
C G K
J O ___

16 PUZZLE

Which number will complete this grid?

2	1	2	7	3	2	4
5	1	4	2	9	2	7
4	1	6	6	2	2	7
1	1	1	6	4	4	2
1	1	4	2	5	0	4
4	1	2	9	3	4	

17 PUZZLE

Which of the numbered pieces fits into the middle of the grid?

5	7	2	1	9	0	3	6	5	7
J	Q	L	C	Y	P	R	A	S	J
2	1	9	0	3	6	5	7	2	1
Q	L	C	Y	■	■	A	S	J	Q
9	0	3	■	■	■	1	9	0	
L	C	Y	■	■	■	J	Q	L	
3	6	5	7	■	■	9	0	3	6
C	Y	P	R	A	S	J	Q	L	C
5	7	2	1	9	0	3	6	5	7
Y	P	R	A	S	J	Q	L	C	Y

1

J Q
2 1 9 0
R A S J
3 6

2

A S
7 2 1 9
C Y P R
6 5

3

J Q
1 9 0 3
R A S J
6 5

4

P R
6 5 7 2
P R A S
2 1

5

L C
3 6 5 7
C Y P R
2 1

Which playing card is missing?

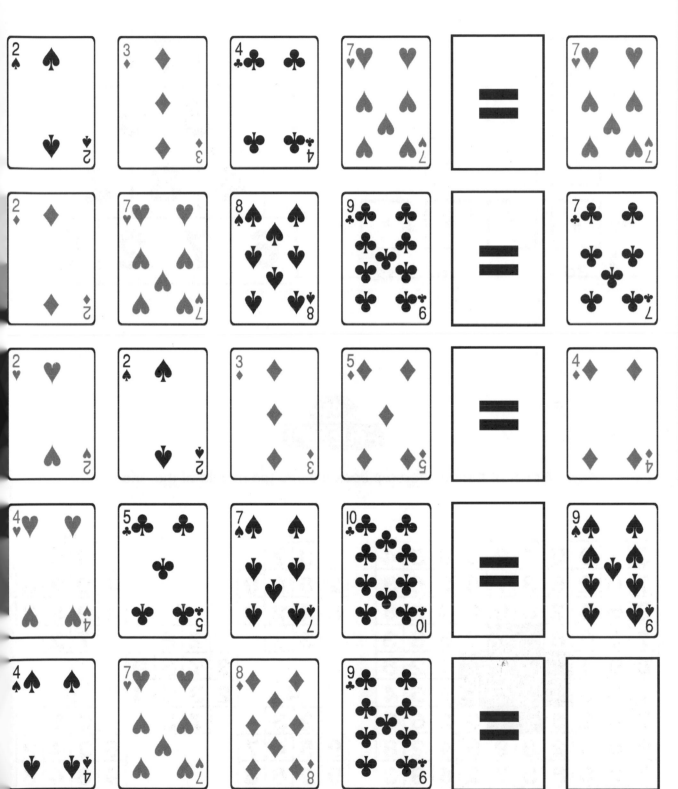

What is the missing value?

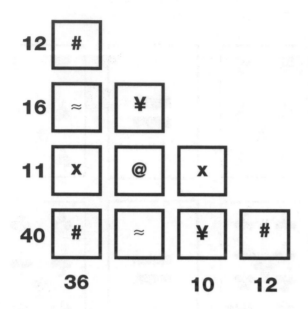

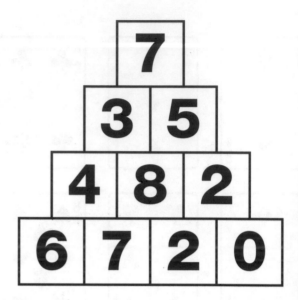

20 PUZZLE

Why is this pyramid correct?

Which of the numbered pieces fits into the middle of the grid?

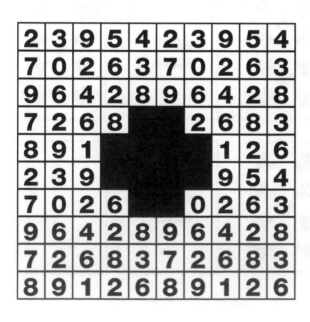

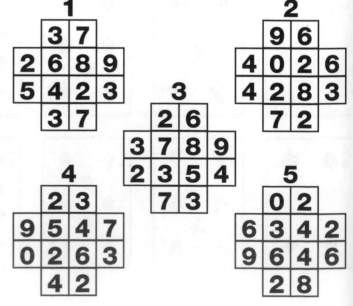

Which playing card completes the puzzle?

 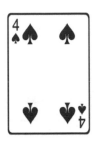  

23
PUZZLE

Which number is the odd one out?

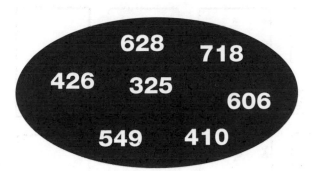

628
718
426
325
606
549
410

24
PUZZLE

What is the time now if it were 2 hours later it would be half as long until midnight as it would be if it were an hour later?

L E V E L

14

Which cards are missing?

PUZZLE 1

Which number is missing?

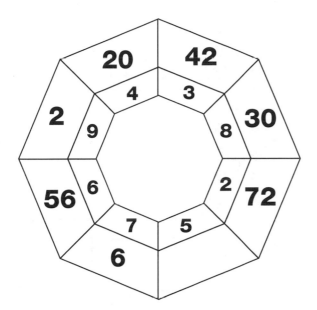

PUZZLE 2

Which number goes in the empty box?

| 5 | 6 | 4 |

| 12 | 2 | |

| 7 | 4 | 6 |

| 8 | 3 | 10 |

PUZZLE 3

Which watch comes next?

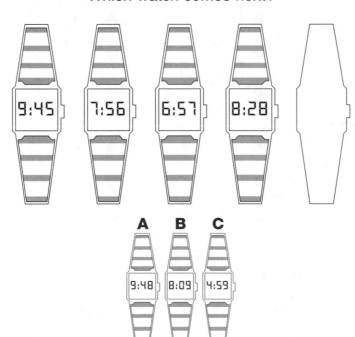

9:45   7:56   6:57   8:28

A   B   C

9:48   8:09   4:59

LEVEL

15

141

Which playing cards are missing?

5 PUZZLE

Which number is missing from the last circle?

  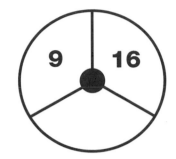

6 PUZZLE

Which of the bottom boxes finishes the sequence?

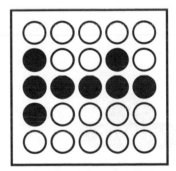 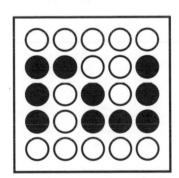 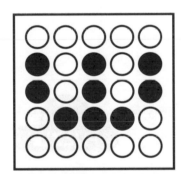

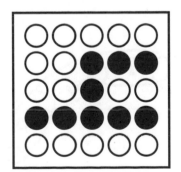 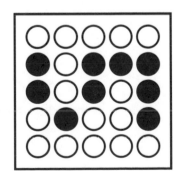 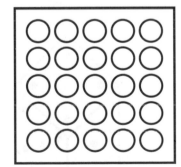

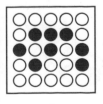 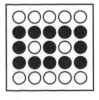 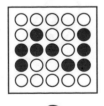 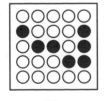 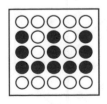 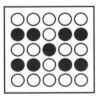

A   **B**   **C**   **D**   **E**   **F**

PUZZLE 7

Which card is missing?

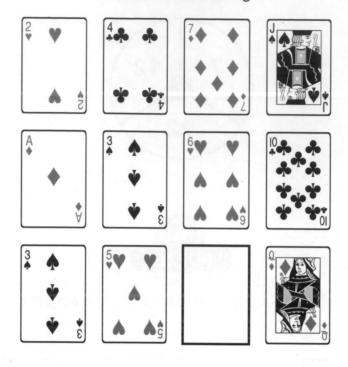

PUZZLE 8

What is the sum of the dots on the hidden faces of these dice?

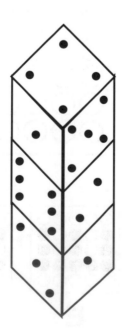

PUZZLE 9

Which number is missing from the chain?

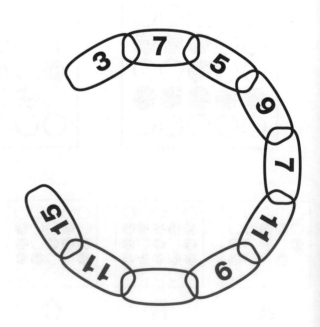

PUZZLE 10

Which numbers need to be placed in the circles in the bottom two boxes?

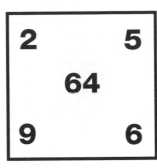
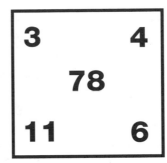

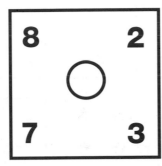
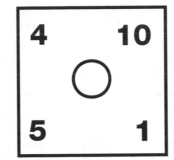

PUZZLE 11

Which number goes in the empty circle?

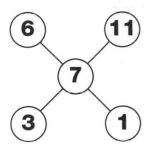
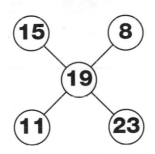
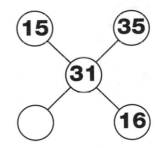

PUZZLE 12

Which number replaces the question mark?

3		7
	?	
4		5

8		4
	20	
4		3

9		4
	22	
7		2

4		5
	14	
2		3

LEVEL

15

Which playing cards are missing from this puzzle?

LEVEL

15

14 PUZZLE

Which letter replaces the blank and completes the sequence?

B	B
F	G
J	L
M	Q
Q	V
T	

15 PUZZLE

Which number goes at the bottom of the column?

5

12

18

23

27

16 PUZZLE

What is missing from the empty ellipse?

I — 31 — E

O — 17 — Y

— 23 — O

17 PUZZLE

Fill in the empty box.

5	5	11
3	8	7

6	10	14
7	10	13

2	10	12
6	7	

LEVEL

15

147

PUZZLE 18

What is missing from the empty segment?

PUZZLE 19

Which letter goes in the middle of the third triangle?

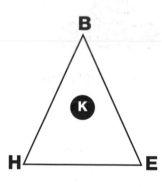

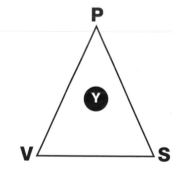

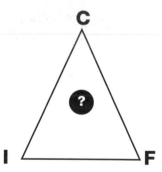

PUZZLE 20

Which letter goes in the empty segment?

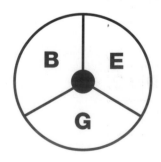

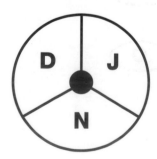

Which letter goes in the empty segment?

Which number replaces the blank and completes the puzzle?

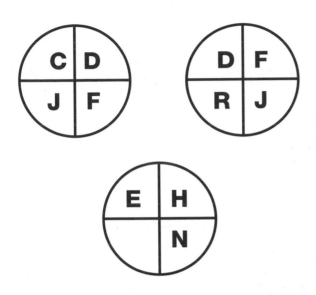

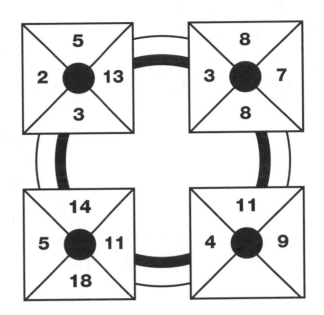

23 PUZZLE

Which of the smaller grids fits into the middle of the larger one?

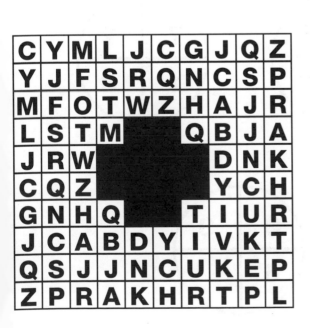

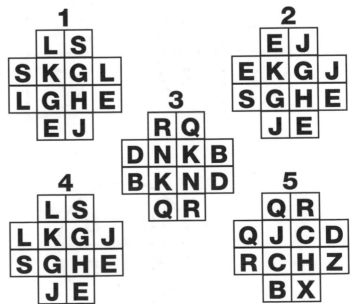

LEVEL

5

PUZZLE 1

Which number is missing from the last grid?

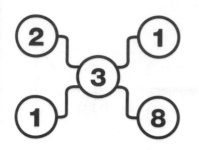 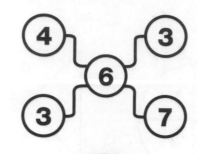 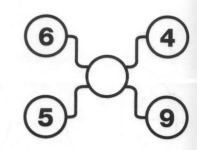

PUZZLE 2

Which card comes next?

     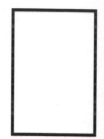

PUZZLE 3

Which number is missing from the last grid?

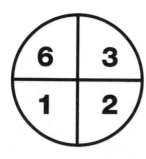  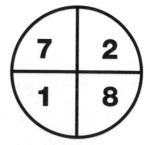

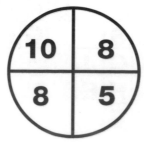 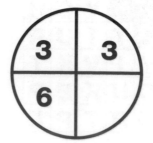

PUZZLE 4

Which number is missing from the empty circle?

PUZZLE 5

Which numbers replaces the blanks?

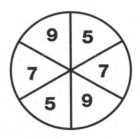

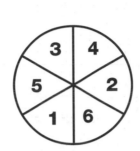

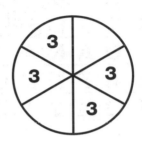

PUZZLE 6

Sisters Janine and Jackie went shopping for new outfits for a wedding. They each bought three items and by coincidence, each spent exactly £222.22. Janine noticed something else – if you look at the price of each item the value in pounds is the square of the pence value.

If one of Janine's items cost £1.01 and one of Jackie's cost £169.13 what are the prices of the other two items?

PUZZLE 7

Which letter is missing from the wheel?

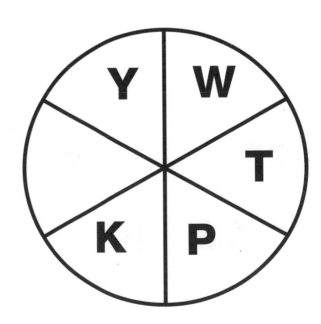

PUZZLE 8

Which of the numbered grids fits into the big one?

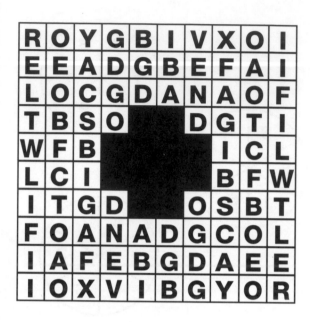

R	O	Y	G	B	I	V	X	O	I
E	E	A	D	G	B	E	F	A	I
L	O	C	G	D	A	N	A	O	F
T	B	S	O			D	G	T	I
W	F	B					I	C	L
L	C	I					B	F	W
I	T	G	D			O	S	B	T
F	O	A	N	A	D	G	C	O	L
I	A	F	E	B	G	D	A	E	E
I	O	X	V	I	B	G	Y	O	R

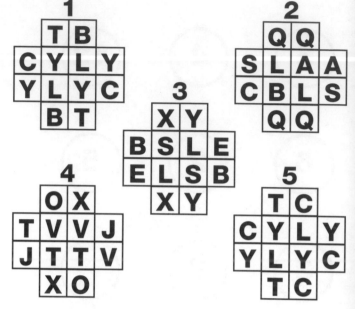

1
T	B		
C	Y	L	Y
Y	L	Y	C
	B	T	

2
		Q	Q
S	L	A	A
C	B	L	S
		Q	Q

3
	X	Y	
B	S	L	E
E	L	S	B
	X	Y	

4
	O	X	
T	V	V	J
J	T	T	V
	X	O	

5
	T	C	
C	Y	L	Y
Y	L	Y	C
	T	C	

PUZZLE 9

Which number completes the wheel?

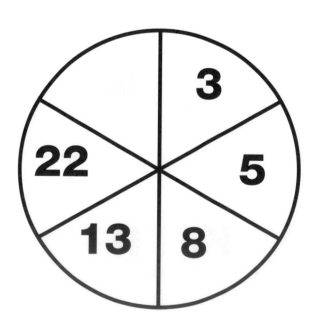

PUZZLE 10

What is missing from the empty square?

M	1	5
O	1	7

V	2	5
I	1	2

T	2	4
L	1	

11 PUZZLE

Which number completes the bottom grid?

1	3	4
5	2	3

6	2	8
7	1	6

4	7	11
11	2	

12 PUZZLE

Which letter goes in the empty square?

D	R	F	
K	H	V	J
B	O	L	
F	S	P	

13 PUZZLE

Complete the wheel by adding the missing number.

14 PUZZLE

What goes in the empty box to complete the puzzle?

O	V	H
17	10	24

M	E	T
18	26	11

F	N	X
24	16	

16

15 PUZZLE

Where is the minute hand pointing to in the bottom clock?

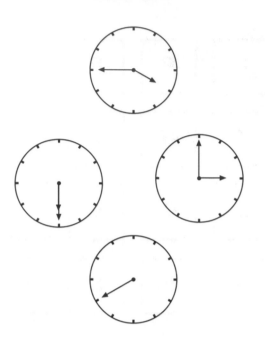

16 PUZZLE

Which number goes in the centre of the bottom right box?

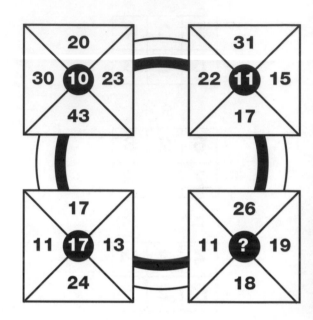

17 PUZZLE

Which of the bottom grids would continue the sequence?

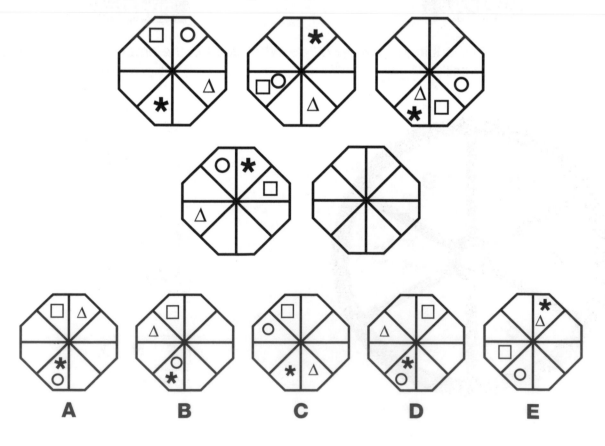

A   B   C   D   E

18 PUZZLE

Which playing cards will fill in the blanks?

PUZZLE 19

Gary writes out a sum for his girlfriend Selina. Although it was wrong he challenged her to change just one symbol to make the sum correct.
Can you see how she did it?

$$1 + 2 - 3 = 139$$

PUZZLE 20

Which letter replaces the blank and completes the sequence?

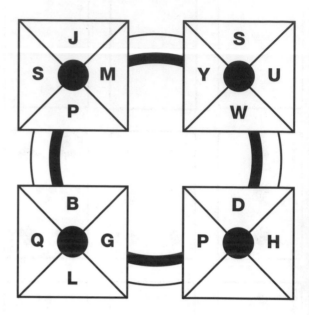

PUZZLE 21

Which figure will come next?

A **B** **C**

PUZZLE 22

Which number will continue this sequence?

42 30 20 12 6

PUZZLE 23

Which number is missing from the last star?

  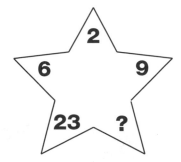

PUZZLE 24

Which shapes are missing?

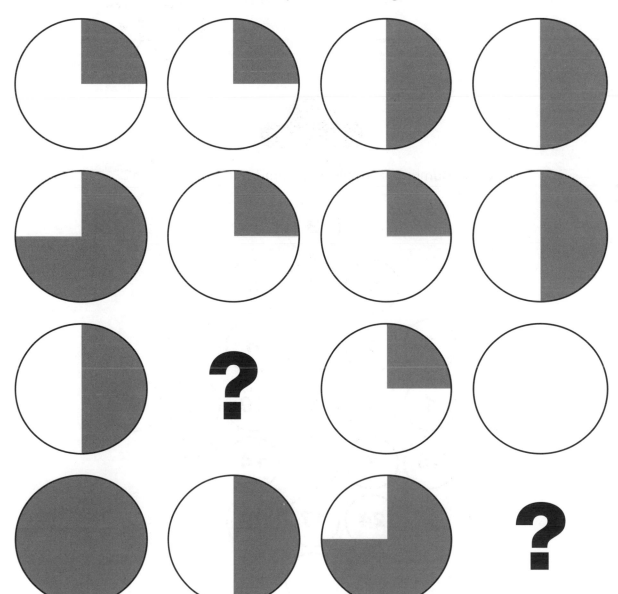

LEVEL

16

25 PUZZLE

Move three matches to form a pattern containing 8 equilateral triangles.

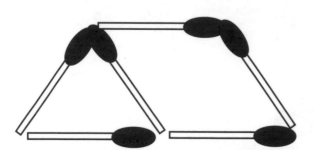

26 PUZZLE

Which number is missing?

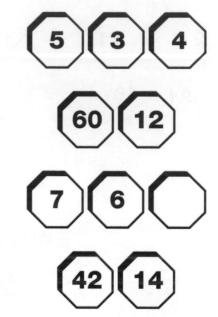

27 PUZZLE

Which numbers are missing from the centre column?

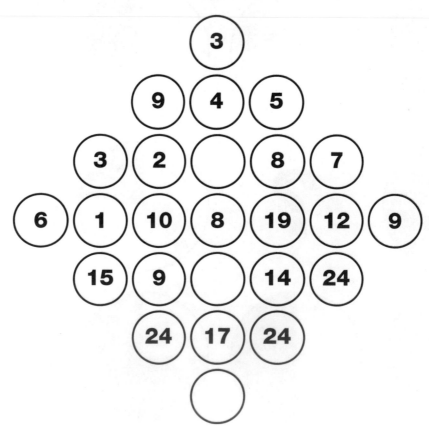

Which of the smaller grids goes in the centre of the large one?

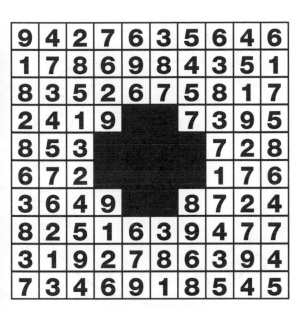

1

```
  3 2
9 4 6 7
3 1 2 3
  8 9
```

2

```
  9 9
2 1 6 7
9 3 1 2
  4 4
```

3

```
  6 6
9 5 3 2
8 7 6 2
  6 3
```

4

```
  4 2
6 8 3 7
2 1 9 4
  2 4
```

5

```
  2 9
8 3 7 6
2 1 4 5
  7 3
```

Which number goes in the centre of the third triangle?

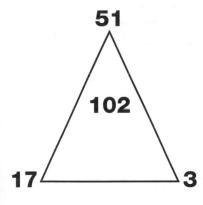 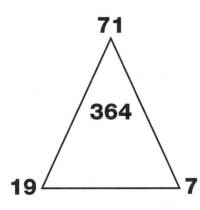 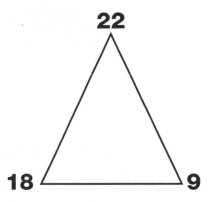

Which number comes next?

PUZZLE 4

Which number is missing?

18	13	26	21
9	266	261	42
14	133	522	37
7		69	74

PUZZLE 5

Which letter completes the chain?

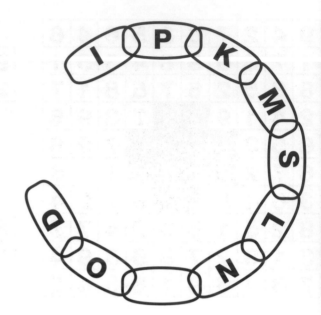

I P K M S L N O D

PUZZLE 6

Which letter is missing from the wheel?

Z A Y J V

PUZZLE 7

Which letter goes in the empty box?

C	I	L
G	M	P

D	Q	S
I	V	X

F	K	R
L	Q	

8 PUZZLE

Which of the smaller pieces will fit into the big grid?

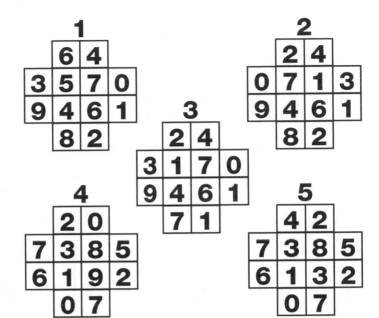

1
```
  6 4
3 5 7 0
9 4 6 1
  8 2
```

2
```
    2 4
0 7 1 3
9 4 6 1
    8 2
```

3
```
    2 4
3 1 7 0
9 4 6 1
    7 1
```

4
```
  2 0
7 3 8 5
6 1 9 2
  0 7
```

5
```
    4 2
7 3 8 5
6 1 3 2
    0 7
```

9 PUZZLE

Which number completes the puzzle?

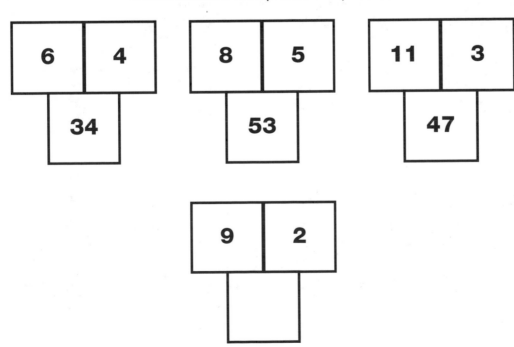

| 6 | 4 |
| 34 | |

| 8 | 5 |
| 53 | |

| 11 | 3 |
| 47 | |

| 9 | 2 |
| | |

17

Which letter is missing from the bottom right hand grid?

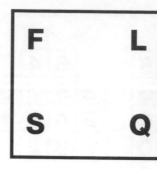

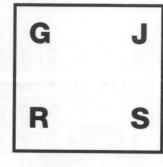

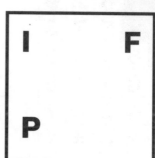

11
PUZZLE

Which of the bottom grids continues the sequence shown on the top line?

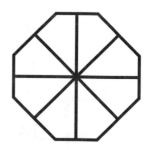

A   **B**   **C**   **D**

LEVEL

Which number goes in the empty circle and completes this puzzle?

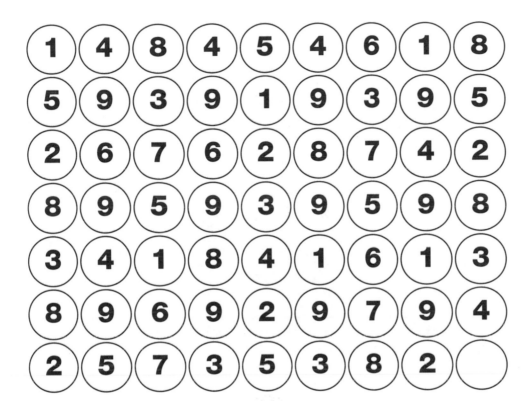

1	4	8	4	5	4	6	1	8
5	9	3	9	1	9	3	9	5
2	6	7	6	2	8	7	4	2
8	9	5	9	3	9	5	9	8
3	4	1	8	4	1	6	1	3
8	9	6	9	2	9	7	9	4
2	5	7	3	5	3	8	2	

What goes in the empty box?

C	R	2	1
Q	W	4	0
L	A	1	3
M	T	3	

Which letter replaces the blank and completes the sequence?

| B |
| C |
| D |
| G |
| |

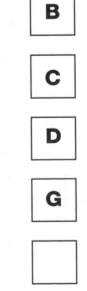

L
E
V
E
L

17

163

PUZZLE 15

Which of the watches on the bottom row continue the sequence shown on the top?

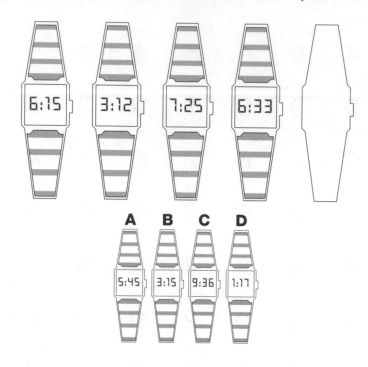

PUZZLE 16

Which of the bottom grids would continue the top sequence?

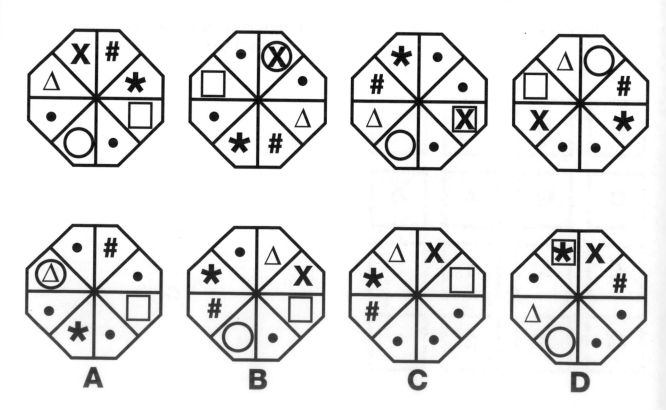

Which numbers are missing?

A **B**

3	9	1
1		2
7		3
7	2	9

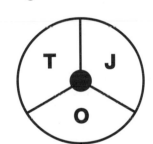

1	9	2
3		0
2		6
3	2	

2	7	0
5		0
4		5
1	9	

18
PUZZLE

Which letter goes in the blank segment?

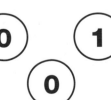

19
PUZZLE

Which number goes in the last circle?

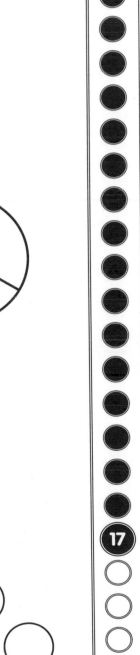

20 PUZZLE

Which number goes at the bottom of the column?

4

9

25

49

121

21 PUZZLE

Which number is missing from the empty box?

2	3	5
7	11	13

2	4	8
12	20	24

3	6	12
18	30	

22 PUZZLE

Which number should go in the empty segment of the wheel?

6

15

7

11

9

23 PUZZLE

What is missing from the empty ellipse?

1 — N — 3

2 — F — 1

2 — C —

166

Mr Jones, the local greengrocer, has lost the weights from his shop scales. He sells pineapples, grapes and apples by weight, but bananas cost 20p each. Mrs Brown wants to buy a pineapple, which Mr Jones will sell to her for the price of the same weight in bananas. He knows that the combinations shown below are correct, so how much will the pineapple cost his customer?

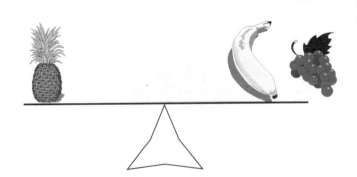

LEVEL

17

Which number is missing from the top of the last star?

PUZZLE 1

Which number is missing from the empty box?

3	6	9
14	8	11

2	4	6
12	8	10

4	8	12
19	11	

PUZZLE 2

What goes in the empty square?

C	G	K
12	10	
X	T	P

PUZZLE 3

Which number begins this sequence?

121

81

49

25

9

PUZZLE 4

Which letter completes the chain?

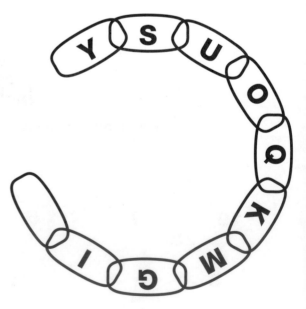

PUZZLE 5

Which number is missing?

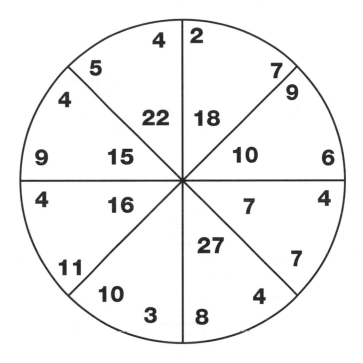

PUZZLE 6

Which two cards from the bottom row continue the sequence shown on the top?

Which two cards complete this sequence?

PUZZLE 8

Which number is missing?

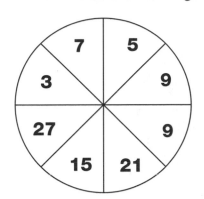

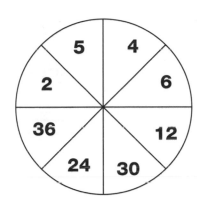

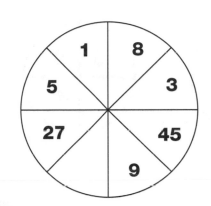

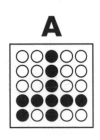

PUZZLE 9

Which of the smaller grids will complete the puzzle?

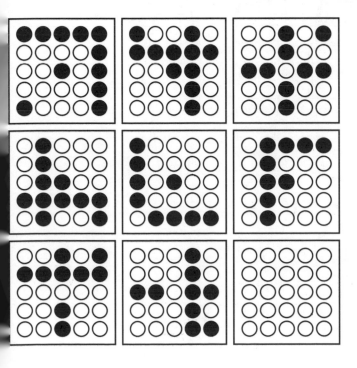

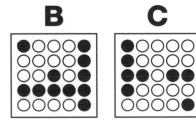

A   **B**   **C**

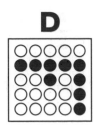
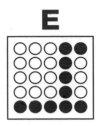
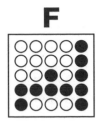

D   **E**   **F**

10 PUZZLE

Which number is missing?

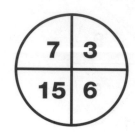
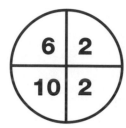
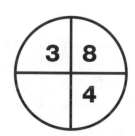

11 PUZZLE

Which number continues the sequence?

5

7

11

19

35

12 PUZZLE

Which of the smaller watches would continue the sequence shown on the top line?

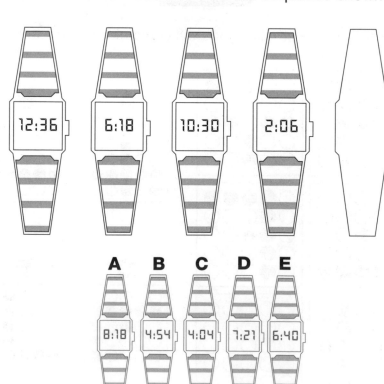

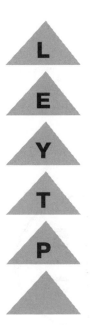

13 PUZZLE

Which of the smaller grids goes in the middle?

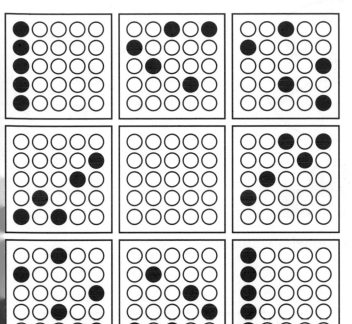

A

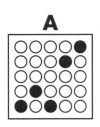

B

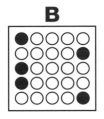

C

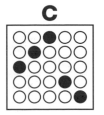

D

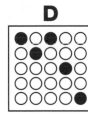

E

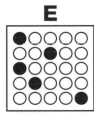

F

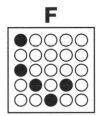

14 PUZZLE

Which number is missing from the empty segment?

7	10
13	6

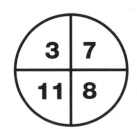

3	7
11	8

10	9
8	2

6	11
16	

15 PUZZLE

Which letter replaces the blank and completes the sequence?

L

E

Y

T

P

LEVEL

PUZZLE 16

Which number is missing from the last circle?

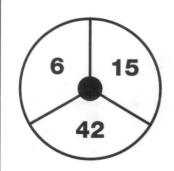

PUZZLE 17

Which watch continues the sequence?

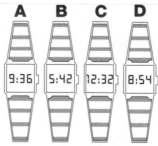

A   B   C   D

PUZZLE 18

Which number is missing?

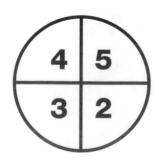

174

19 PUZZLE

What time will be on the next watch?

20 PUZZLE

Which number is missing from the third triangle?

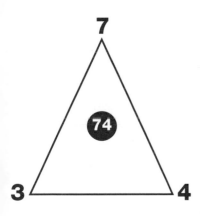

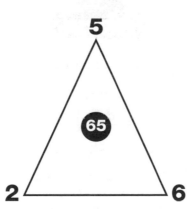

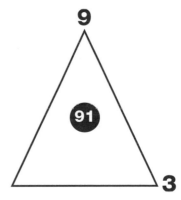

21 PUZZLE

Which number is missing?

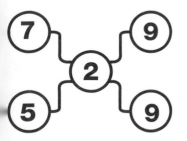

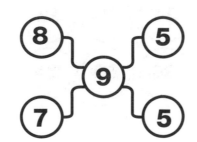

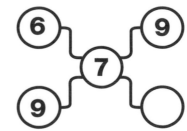

PUZZLE 1

Which number is missing from the web.

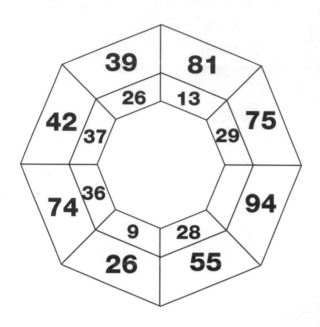

PUZZLE 2

Which number goes in the empty square?

7	3	6
45	5	32

5	8	4
21	60	

PUZZLE 3

Which number goes in the bottom circle?

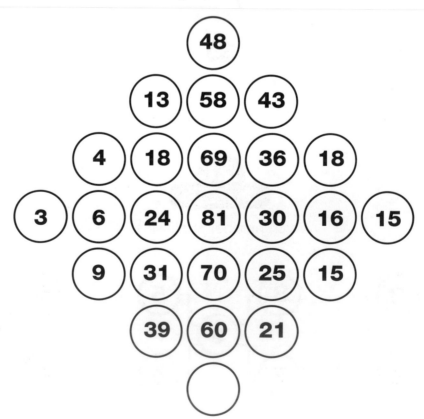

PUZZLE 4

Which number is missing from the bottom grid?

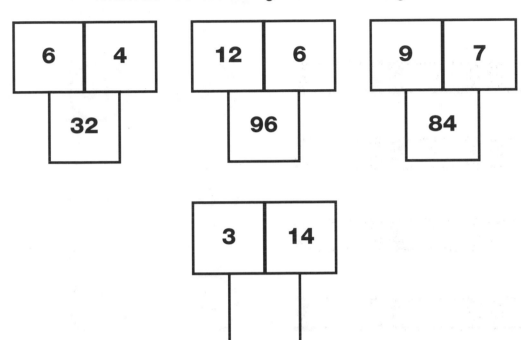

6	4
32	

12	6
96	

9	7
84	

3	14

PUZZLE 5

Draw the correct number of circles in the blank square.

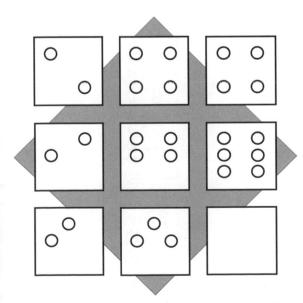

PUZZLE 6

Which number comes next?

10
15
25
35

PUZZLE 7

What goes in the empty box?

24	W	5
20	S	9
16	O	13
11		18

PUZZLE 8

Which number is missing from the empty circle?

4	10	28
6	16	46
3	7	

PUZZLE 9

Which letter replaces the blank and completes the puzzle?

P	C	H
D	L	K
N		E

PUZZLE 10

Which number comes next?

5
9
17
33

11 PUZZLE

Which letter goes in the empty box?

C	B	F
G	G	L
K	L	R
O	Q	

12 PUZZLE

Which number continues this sequence?

3

8

18

38

☐

13 PUZZLE

Which letter goes in the empty circle?

B

T   X   F

P   Z   D   B   J

L   V   P   T   H   F   N

H   R   ( )   J   R

D   N   V

Z

I J K L M N O P

PUZZLE 14

What time should the blank watch be showing?

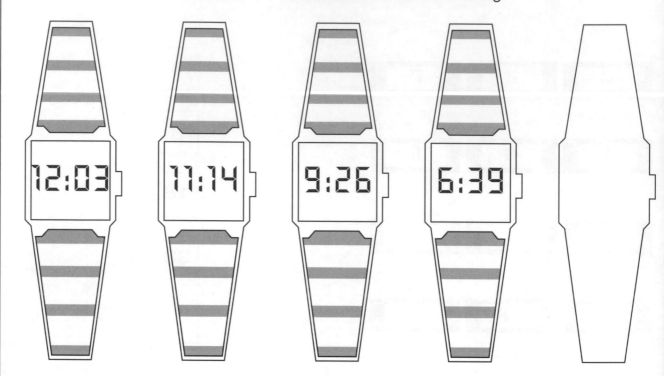

12:03   11:14   9:26   6:39

PUZZLE 15

What goes in the empty circle?

1   Q   O

1   H   9

2   C   ( )

PUZZLE 16

Which number is missing?

7	11	3
6	14	4
5	7	3
2	7	

LEVEL

9

180

Four men went to the building supplies centre to buy some tools for the workmen on the building sites they were in charge of. Chris buys 3 screwdrivers, 4 hammers and 5 saws for the men on his building site at a total cost of £9.70. Carl buys 4 screwdrivers, 5 hammers and 3 saws for his carpenters at a total cost of £9. Charlie's £8.90 bought 5 screwdrivers, 3 hammers and 4 saws. Colin, who is in charge of a small building site has less money to spend but still needs 1 screwdriver, 1 hammer and a saw. How much did he have to spend?

Chris

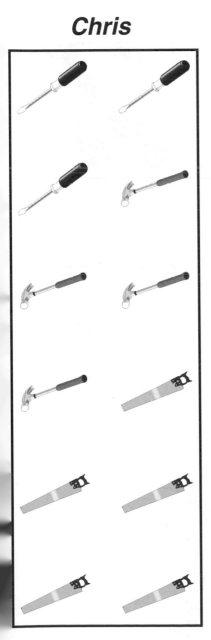

Charlie

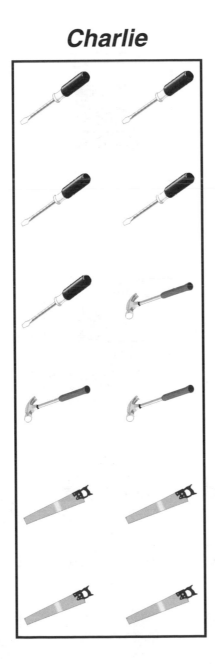

Carl

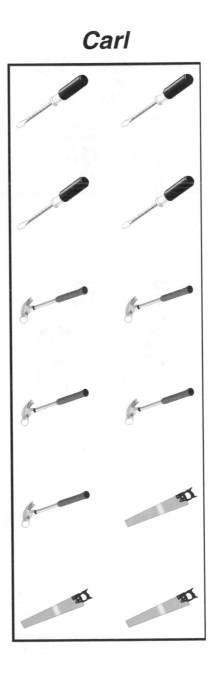

PUZZLE

Which of the six smaller boxes finishes this sequence?

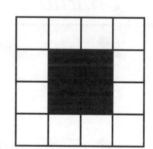

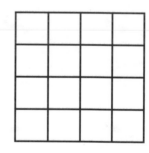

A

B

C

D

E

F

PUZZLE 1

Which letters replace the blanks and complete the sequence?

Y	O	V	M
K	B	P	A
M	D	R	
Z	P	W	

PUZZLE 2

Which number goes in the empty box?

3	7	9
5	8	11
1	6	7
2	1	

PUZZLE 3

Which letter is missing?

 B   D   G

 K   T   K

 C   P

PUZZLE 4

Which number is missing from the middle of the circle?

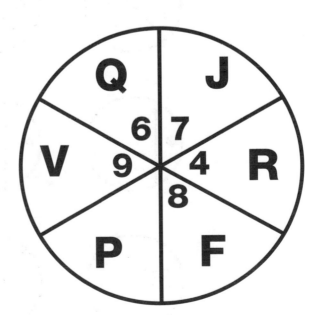

PUZZLE 5

Which number replaces the question mark?

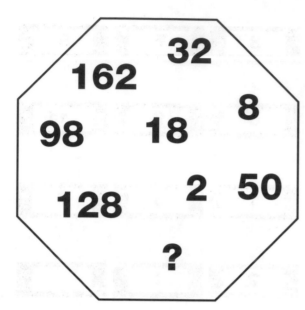

PUZZLE 6

Which number comes next?

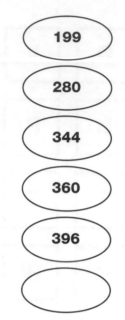

199

280

344

360

396

PUZZLE 7

Draw the contents of the empty circle.

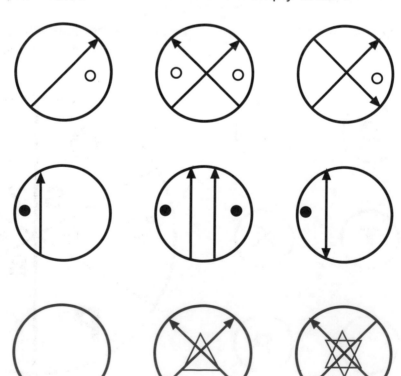

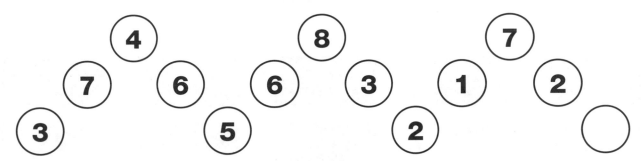

8 PUZZLE

Which number goes in the empty circle and completes the puzzle?

④ ⑧ ⑦
⑦ ⑥ ⑥ ③ ① ②
③ ⑤ ② ◯

9 PUZZLE

Which numbers complete the last two grids?

7	8	8
9		0
9		8
4	6	0

A

1	9	2
9		0
7		6
2		9

B

8	8	8
2		1
7		8
6		7

10 PUZZLE

Which number is missing?

3	7	8	6	1	9	1	2	9
5	8	1	3	2	8	3	2	6
4	1	7	2	5	7	4	4	9
7	3	4	9	7	5	2	5	4
6	6	9	1	3	8	8	7	2
1	6	1	8	6	3	7	2	2
6	9	6	3	8	8	3	2	

PUZZLE 11

Which domino completes the pattern?

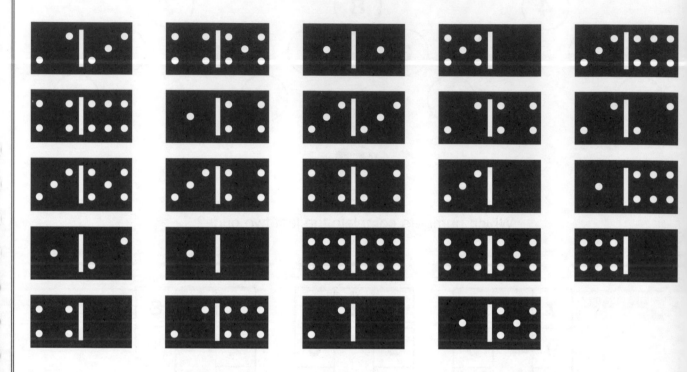

PUZZLE 12

Which of the three letters at the bottom fit into the top grid?

PUZZLE 13

Which letter replaces the blank and completes the sequence?

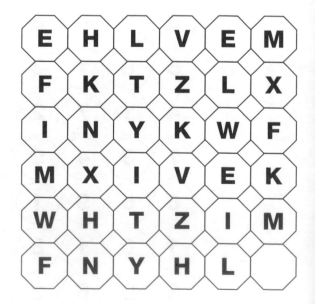

14 PUZZLE

Which number logically fits into the empty square?

2	9	3	7	6	8
7	1	5	2	0	7
8	5	4	2	9	3

8	8	2	3	9	8
6	5	1	5	4	8
3	5	6	9	5	

15 PUZZLE

Which letter replaces the blank and completes the sequence?

B	D	G	B	A	F
G	D	C	H	H	D
E	F	G	F	E	B

F	D	C	F	H	H
G	D	A	C	C	H
D	C	G	G	F	

16 PUZZLE

Which shape is the odd one out?

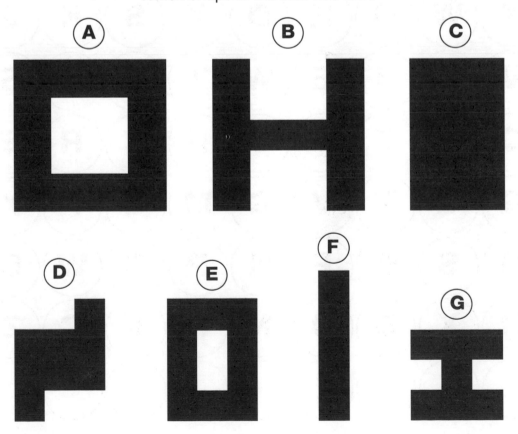

LEVEL

Complete the last row of the puzzle.

B	J	F	F	L	Z	T	R	F
K	D	G	K	A	S	S	D	I
C	H	J	B	R	T	C	J	Q
I	H	C	Q	U	B	K	P	Z
G	D	P	V	Z	L	N	A	B
E	N	W	Y	M	M	B	Z	Q
M	X	X	N	L	C	Y	R	L
Y	W	O	K	D	X	S	K	J
V	P	J	E	W	T	J	K	S
Q	H	F	V	U	H	L	R	E
G	G	T	V	G	M	Q	F	X
H	S	W	F	N	P	G	W	B
R	X	D	O	N	H	V	C	Z

20

SOLUTIONS

1 - 6
In each square the bottom segment equals the sum of the other 3 segments.

2 - C
In each row, the sum of the centre letter equals the sum of the left and right hand letters.

3 - 71
Add the first two numbers together to get the third, repeating around the grid.

4 - 23
In columns, add the first three numbers together to get the figure in the bottom box.

5 - P
In each circle, letters move clockwise by increasing steps.

6 - 4
Numbers in each column add up to 9.

7 -

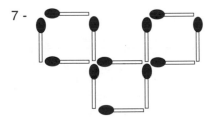

8 - X
Letters advance by 4, 5, 6 and 7.

9 - U
In columns, the value of the bottom letter equals the sum of the values of the other two.

10 - 8
Working in rows, add the left and centre numbers together to give the result on the right.

11 - 9
In rows, add the left and centre figures to get the right hand number.

12 - 3
Working in rows, the figure on the right equals half the difference between the left and central numbers.

13 - 1
Taking the top and bottom lines separately, add the left and centre numbers, then subtract the right hand number to give the figure in the middle.

14 - 4
Numbers in each row add up to 14.

15 -

Working in columns, as you move down, one feature is removed with each step, and the smile alternates with the frown.

16 - 5
In rows, double the left and centre digits and add together to give the right hand figure.

17 - 23
Moving across each row, from top to bottom, the numbers follow the sequence of prime numbers.

18 - 2
In each square, the sum of the 3 outer numbers divided by the central number always equals 6.

19 - 1 = P, 2 = J
All the other letters contain straight lines only.

20 - 36
Segments in the right hand half equal the squares of the diagonally opposing segments on the left.

21 - R
Starting in the top left of each figure and moving clockwise, the letters ascend the alphabet

in steps given in the centre value.

22 - M
Each centre letter is the midpoint between the pairs of letters in the diagonal lines.

23 - 11
Working in rows, halve the first number, double the middle number and add them together to give the right hand number.

24 - 5
Working in rows, the first three* numbers add up to the right hand number. In the next line, the three numbers to the right add up to the left hand number, etc. etc.

25 - No.
As the water level rises the pointer moves towards 'Drought'.

26 - X
The letters in the central column come midway in the alphabet between the left and right hand numbers.

27 - P
The numbers between pairs of letters equal the sum of the numerical values of the letters on either side.

28 - Ace (of any suit)
Taking the vertical, horizontal and 2 diagonal lines through the centre of the square, the sum of the values at the ends of the lines equal 12, the value of the centre card.

29 - E & S
Starting on the left and going down, then up the right column, letters advance in steps of two.

30 -

Working in rows from left to

SOLUTIONS

right, the dot moves anticlockwise by one segment, then
clockwise by three.

31 - 1
In each circle, the bottom
number equals the sum of the
squares of the top two numbers.

32 - K
In each star, the letters run
clockwise in alphabetical order,
in steps of 3 for the left hand
star, 4 for the centre and 2 for
the right hand star.

33 - W & E
In each circle, add 5 to the
value of the top left letter to give
the bottom left letter, and then
add 2 to the top right to give the
bottom right.

34 - 7
Working in rows, the central
number equals the sum of the
left and right hand numbers.

35 - 17
The chain follows the sequence
of prime numbers.

36 - J
In rows, the value of the right
hand letter equals the difference
between the values of the left
and centre letters.

37 - 23
Starting in the top left corner
and moving clockwise in a spiral, add 3 to get the next value,
then 2, then 1, etc.

LEVEL 2

1 -
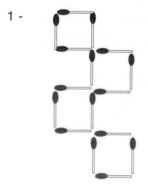

2 - It will rise.

3 - 48
Numbers advance by 2, 4, 8
and 16.

4 - 3
In each row, add the left and the
right hand numbers and divide
by 2 to get the central value.

5 - U
In each row, add the numerical
value of the left and centre
letters to give the right hand
letter.

6 - 9
Each row, column and diagonal
adds up to 15.

7 - 2
Add the numerical values of
each pair of letters and write the
answer, as two separate digits
in the boxes underneath.

8 - G
Working clockwise around each
star, letters increase in steps
given by the numerical value of
the central figure.

9 - Z
Letters advance in steps of 12,
returning to the start of the
alphabet after Z.

10 - R
In columns, add the numerical
value of the top and middle
letters to give the bottom letters.

11 - 2
In each triangle, add the lower
two digits and multiply by the
top digit to give the value in the
centre.

12 - 7 -
In each line, the central number
equals the left hand number
and double the right hand
number.

13 - H
Going clockwise around each
square, the letters increase in
value in steps presented by the
central square.

14 -
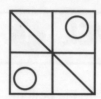

Working in rows, the central
figure is made from superimposing the left and right hand
figures.

15 - 81
As you go down, subtract the
sum of the separate digits in
each number from itself to give
the next number.

16 - A
In each row, from left to right,
the black circle moves clockwise around each corner, the
hash moves one place down
and the triangle moves anticlockwise around the central 4
squares.

17 - 7
Add the top figures together,
then the bottom ones. The
central figure is the difference
between these two answers.

18 - 4

19 - 14
Starting on the left, double each
number and add two to give the
value in the corresponding
segment in the circle to the
right.

20 -
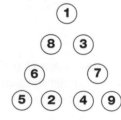

21 - 8
All vertical and diagonal lines
through the centre add up
to 14.

22 - 8
In each circle, the sum of the
odd numbers plus one equals
the sum of the even numbers.

SOLUTIONS

23 - 34
Starting at 3 and moving clockwise, double the preceding number and subtract 2.

24 - 72cm

25 - 13
Moving clockwise, each segment equals the sum of the previous two segments.

26 - T
Multiply the numerical value of the left hand letter by the right hand letter to give the central figure.

27 - 13
Going down the columns, moving left to right, numbers follow the sequence of prime numbers.

28 - C
Working in rows from left to right, the @ moves 1 place clockwise in the central 4 squares, the ∆ moves 2 places clockwise around the outside of the square, while the ∗ moves 2 places anticlockwise.

29 - 7
In each circle, the sum of the digits equals 34.

30 - S
The numerical value of the bottom letters equals the sum of the numerical values of the top two letters.

31 - Z
Starting from C and moving clockwise letters advance alternately 5 and 4 places.

32 - M
Working in columns, the bottom letter equals the sum of the top and centre letters.

LEVEL 3

1 - G
In each triangle the numerical value of the lower left letter

increases by the value of the top letter to give the lower right letter.

2 - 29
The sum of the numerical values of the three letters.

3 - K
Letters in the left hand column move through the alphabet, skipping letters written without curves, letters in the right hand column skip letters with curves.

4 - 6 Painters.

5 - F
In each circle, the sum of the numerical values of opposite segments adds up to the same figure - 16 for the left hand circle, 17 for the top and 18 for the bottom.

6 - 60
Multiply the figures at the opposite ends of the central circle to give the same answer.

7 - 9
The four corners add up to 35, as do the four centre figures on each side of the square.

8 - 6
The numbers in each square, including the middle one, add up to 15.

9 - 3
Working in columns, divide the top value by the centre to give the bottom figure.

10 - 12
As you go down each pair of numbers, the left hand value equals the sum of the numbers above and the right hand value equals the difference of the pair of numbers above.

11 - 2
The figures in each row add up to 11.

12 - W
In rows from left to right each

letter represents the numerical value of the first 9 prime numbers.

13 - Ace of Hearts
In each row the sum of the red cards equals the sum of the black cards, with one card from each suit in every line.

14 - 5
The sum of the numerical values of the letters are written on the bottom two points of each star as a two digit number.

15 - T
Letters are arranged in alphabetical order, skipping any letters written with curved lines.

16 - 8
The centre value equals the difference between the left and right hand numbers.

17 - 5
The product of the numbers in opposite segments always equals 60.

18 - F
Working in columns, subtract the value of the middle letter from the value of the top letter.

19 - 22
The centre number equals the sum of the bottom two digits minus the top digit.

20 - 43
Moving clockwise the numbers increase by 2, 3, 5, 7, 11 etc. — the sequence of prime numbers.

21 - F
Moving clockwise, letters decrease in value from U in steps of 1, 2, 3, 4 and 5.

22 - 2
In each circle subtract the right hand digit from the left hand digit, then subtract a further one to give the lower digit.

23 - 6
The sum of the values around

191

the edge of the puzzle add up to the centre number.

24 - 3
The two digit numbers in alternate boxes represent the sum of the alphabetical value of the left hand letter in the box above and the reverse alphabetical value of the right hand letter.

25 - T
Letters in opposite segments of the circle are the same distance from the start of the alphabet as the other letter is from the end.

26 - 6
Working in rows, add the first and second numbers, then deduct 1 to give the right hand number.

27 - 8
The sequence follows the formula - double the previous number then add 1, etc.

28 - A = 12, B = 25,
They are the only even number or only odd number in each ellipse.

29 - 4
In each column of three the numbers add up to 16.

30 - 5
In each grid numbers move clockwise in steps given by the central number.

31 - E
In each row, subtract the numerical value of the middle letter from the left hand letter to give the right hand letter.

32 - L
Letters at opposite ends of each line come in pairs – one is the same distance from the start of the alphabet as the other is from the end.

33 - 16 years old.

34 - 26

Going clockwise, numbers represent the sequence of prime numbers multiplied by 2.

35 - O
In each box, multiply the numerical values of the letters, and write the three-figure result in the lower half.

36 - 3
Figures in the centre column equal the sum of the numbers in the right and left.

37 - Q
In each circle the letters move clockwise in increments of 7 for the top left circle through to 3 for the bottom right circle.

LEVEL 4

1 - C

2 - 10
In rows, the centre number equals the difference between the left and right hand numbers.

3 - 3
Add the numerical values of the pairs of letters and write the two digit result in the boxes below.

4 -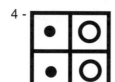

Working in rows, the figure on the right is formed by superimposing the left hand figure rotated 90° clockwise and the centre figure rotated 90° anticlockwise.

5 - 4
In each figure, the sum of the left hand digits divided by the sum of the right hand digits gives the central value.

6 - O
Starting bottom left and moving clockwise in a spiral, letters advance by 9 places, then 8, 7, 6, etc.

7 - 25%

8 - 21
Numbers increase down the row by 5, then 4, 3, etc.

9 - 2 & 0
The digits under each group of letters represent the value of the left hand letter and the reverse alphabetical value of the right hand letter, written as a two digit number.

10 - 19
The figures in the central column equal the sum of the numbers in each corresponding row.

11 - O
Working from left to right, letters in corresponding positions on each triangle advance by 7, 6 or 5 places as you move to the right.

12 - 5
Working in rows, multiply the average of the left and right hand numbers by three to give the middle number.

13 - P
In each diagram, the numerical value of each letter plus the numerical value of the letter below it adds up to the same number.

14 - 14
Starting in the top left and moving between circles in a W shape, numbers in corresponding segments increase in value by 2, 3, 4 and 5.

15 - Y
In each circle, starting with the top left letter, move 10 places forward to give the top right figure, and move another 10 places forward to give the bottom letter.

16 - 2
Working in columns, multiply the top and bottom values to get a 2 figure result, written in the 2 central squares.

SOLUTIONS

17 -

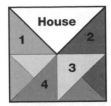

18 - R
Taking rows across each group letters increase by 2, 3, 4, 5 and then 6.

19 - 49
The sum of the digits at corresponding positions on each triangle equals 100.

20 - 54
For each box, the number enclosed by the central box equals the sum of the squares of the other three numbers.

21 - Seven of Hearts
In rows, add the left and central card values to give the value of the right hand card value. The suit of the left card is the same as that of the right hand card.

22 - Q
Starting at the top of each triangle, letters progress clockwise in increments given by the central number plus 2.

23 - 5 mechanics, with a little time left over.

24 - 4

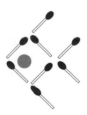

25 - 42
As you go down, double the previous number and subtract 10.

26 - 54 or 6
Segments on the left equal the values in the opposite segments multiplied by three.

27 - 3
In each grid, add the top 6-digit number to the middle number to give the bottom result.

28 -

29 - A
Using the numerical values of the letters, each set of four diagonally opposite letters equals 19.

30 - 1 = L, 2 = E
All other letters are written with three lines.

LEVEL 5

1 - 8 biscuits.

2 - 11 & 5
Alternate numbers increase by 2, the others decrease by 1.

3 - 677
Square each value and add 1 to get the next number.

4 - L
Add the numerical values of the bottom two letters and divide by the numerical value of the top letter to give the value of the centre letter.

5 - 66
Working from left to right, double the previous number and subtract 2.

6 - E
Going clockwise letters increase in value by the value of the centre letter.

7 - 13
Starting at the top, add the two numbers together to give the left hand number underneath. The right hand number is the same as the left hand number above.

8 - K
Moving clockwise in alternate sections, letters advance by 6 or 5 places.

9 - 23
Working clockwise, numbers increase by 2, 3 and 4 in a repeating sequence.

10 - 3
The difference in the numbers in each segment equals the numerical value of the letter in the opposite segment.

11 - V
Starting top left and moving clockwise in a spiral, letters advance in steps of 2, 3, 4, 5 etc.

12 - 1/4 of the original amount.

13 - 35
Numbers advance in steps of 7, 8, 9 and 10.

14 - 4
In each figure the middle value equals the difference between the products of the top pair of numbers and the bottom pair.

15 - Yes
The bottom left turns anticlockwise, while all the others turn clockwise.

16 - 14
Working in rows, multiply the left and right hand numbers together and add 2 to give the centre value.

17 - 13
In each circle the lower number equals the average of the top two numbers.

18 - D
Working in columns, one cross is removed at each step, first from one side of the pattern, then the opposite side.

19 - D
On each watch the digits add up to 15.

20 - 2
For each circle multiply the top two numbers together to give a 2 digit value, written in the bottom segments.

SOLUTIONS

21 - 4
Starting at the top, the right hand number equals the left hand number plus 6, in the next line add 5, then 4, 3, 2 and 1.

22 - A
Moving from left to right, one dark segment moves 1 place clockwise while the other moves 2 places anticlockwise.

23 - 19
In each circle, going clockwise, alternate even numbers increase in steps of 2, odd numbers increase in steps of 4.

24 - 2
In each row, divide the left hand value by the centre value to get the right hand number.

25 -

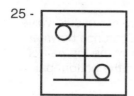

Working in rows from left to right, add the elements of the first two boxes to give the figure on the right.

26 - 8
In each square, multiply the top and bottom numbers then subtract the left and right hand numbers, the result is 40 each time.

27 - 36
In rows, multiply the left and centre numbers then subtract the smaller of the numbers to give the right hand value.

28 - M
Going clockwise move forward 5 places, then back 3, missing out all the vowels.

29 - I
Taking the numerical values of the letters in each figure, subtract the right hand numbers from the left hand numbers on the same line to give the central number.

30 - 15
Each segment in the lower right box equals the sum of the values in the corresponding segments of the other squares.

31 - 2
The numbers in each line of 3 circles, going through the centre, add up to 15.

32 - 10
The values of the points of the central star equal the sums of the values of the corresponding points of the left and right hand stars.

LEVEL 6

1 - 6
In rows the right hand digit equals double the difference between the left and the centre.

2 - J
Letters move clockwise in steps of 10.

3 - 14
Double the numbers in the top left circle to give the values in the lower left circle. Double the numbers in the top right circle to give the values in the lower right circle. The difference between corresponding values are put in the last remaining circle.

4 - 19
The numbers, starting at 2 and going clockwise around each circle, represent the first 9 prime numbers.

5 -

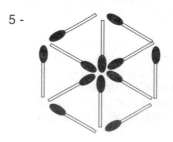

6 - Y
Going clockwise, the letters in alternate segments advance 6.

7 - 6
Numbers in each row add up to 26.

8 - 10
In each circle, add the top 2 numbers and subtract the lower right number to give the lower left number.

9 - 7
Add together the numbers on the outside of each segment and put the result at the centre of the opposite segment.

10 -

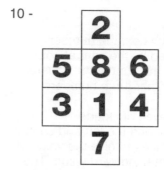

Other answers may also be correct.

11 - W
Letters on the left descend in steps of four. The values of the letters on the right equal the values of the letters on the left plus three, then minus three, etc.

12 - X
In rows letters in the first line increase by steps of 5 from left to right, the second row in steps of 4, the next by three and the bottom line by 2.

13 - 49
Square the values in the segments on the left half, and put the results in the opposite segment on the right.

14 - 24 & 2
Each segment in the lower left circle equals the sum of the corresponding segments in top circles. The numbers in the bottom right circle are the sum of the even numbers in the top circles, minus the odd numbers.

SOLUTIONS

15 - 7
In each circle, multiply the upper left number by 2 and subtract 1 to give the upper right number. Then multiply the original number by 3 and subtract 1 to get the bottom number.

16 - A = 127, B = 56
All other numbers are divisible by 9.

17 - 7
Starting at the top left and working down, and bottom right and working up, add the left hand number to the right hand number and put this answer in the centre column reading downwards.

18 - 14
Numbers on corresponding points of each triangle progress by increasing steps, add 6 then 7 for the top, 5 and 6 for the bottom left and then 7 and 8 for the bottom right.

19 - H
In the first box, starting with the top left, letters advance by a decreasing amount, starting with 6, then 5, 4, etc. The second box advances by 7, 6, 5, etc. and the third box by 8, 7, 6, etc.

20 - 29
As you go down each block of two, the right hand number is duplicated in the left hand square below, and the right hand number equals the sum of the two squares above.

21 - 15
In each circle, the lower left value equals the sum of the numerical values of the letters and the top right value equals the difference in the letter values.

22 - 8
In each diagram the central value equals the difference between the product of the top two numbers and bottom two numbers.

23 - 75
Each shape contains the same numbers multiplied by 3, 4 and 5.

24 - W
In each circle add the numerical values of the upper two letters to give the numerical value of the bottom letter.

25 - G
In each circle, going clockwise, alternate letters increase in value by 3 steps for the left hand circle, 4 for the upper and 5 for the lower circle.

26 - D
In each row, divide the numerical value of the left hand letter by the number in the centre column to give the numerical value of the right hand letter.

27 - 152
As you move clockwise multiply the previous number by 2 and add 2, 3, 4, 5 and 6.

28 - 3
Working in rows the central figure equals the difference in the squares of the left and right hand numbers.

29 - B
Moving across each row from left to right, the # appears in alternate boxes, rotating 1/4 turn around the central 4 squares. The O moves to the right on the top row, then down 1 space and to the left. The * moves to each corner up, down to the left, up then down to the right.

 LEVEL 7

1 - 42
Divide each circle into left and right halves. The top right value equals the sum of the left hand numbers, the middle right value equals the product of the left hand numbers and the bottom right hand value equals the sum of the squares of the left hand numbers.

2 - 32
Working downwards, square the numbers 0, 1, 2, 3 and 4 and multiply by 2.

3 - M
Starting from A alternate letters increase in steps of 3, the other letters, starting from G increase in steps of 2.

4 - 10
Going clockwise, the values increase equal increments and move 90° clockwise each step.

5 - D
The lines along each half domino add up to the number of dots shown on the right hand side.

6 - A
Add the reverse alphabetical value of the bottom two letters of each triangle and subtract the reverse alphabetical value of the top letter to give the value of the middle letter in alphabetical order.

7 - 236
Working in columns from top to bottom, on the left, multiply each value by 2 then subtract 2 to give the next number. In the centre column by 3 and the right hand column by 4.

8 - 2
Starting with the digits to the top and left move in lines of three digits subtracting the centre digit to give the bottom and right figures.

9 - 2
Add the top 2 digits in each group and multiply the centre, the result is written in the bottom circles.

10 - 6
Starting in the top left of each figure, numbers increase in a clockwise direction by the value given in the central circle.

SOLUTIONS

11 - 4
In each column, the sum of the three smaller figures equals the larger figure.

12 - 6
The centre figure is the product of the left and right numbers, minus 1.

13 - 1 = M, 2 = J
The numerical values of No. 1 are divisible by 3, in No. 2 the numbers are divisible by 4.

14 - 51
Working in rows, invert the digits in the left and right hand numbers and add them together to give the central figure.

15 - Five of Clubs
In rows, add together the values of the first four cards to get a 2 digit number. Add these together to give the value of the right hand card. The suit of this card is the same as the card to the left with the highest value.

16 - 68
In each circle, divide the difference between the top and right hand numbers by 4 to give the left hand value.

17 - 168
Subtract 4 then multiply each number by 3 to give the next number.

18 - M
Taking the numerical value of the letters each row and column adds up to 27.

19 - U
Taking all 3 groups together, letters increase in value in rows from left to right by 3 for the top row, 4 for the middle and 5 for the bottom row.

20 - F
In columns, the central number equals the sum of the numerical value of the top and bottom letters.

21 - 12
Starting from the top, subtract 2 then add 7 and continue this sequence.

22 - Z
In rows, add the numerical value of left and centre letters to give the value of the right hand letter.

23 - 21
In each grid, add up the 4 numbers at the corners and write the result downwards in the centre column.

24 - 30
In each circle, multiply the two upper numbers and subtract 10 to give the lower value.

25 - B
Divide the numerical value of the left hand letter by the numerical value of the right hand letter to give the value of the lower letter.

26 - 25
The larger numbers are the squares of the numbers in the opposite segments of the circle.

27 - 1
The figures in the right hand column equal the difference between the numbers in the left and centre columns.

28 - M
Starting at the bottom left and moving anticlockwise, letters progress through the alphabet in steps of 2, then 3, etc. etc. returning to the beginning of the alphabet whenever Z is reached.

29 -

Working in rows, rotate the left hand figure by a 1/4 turn clockwise to give the central figure, and 1/4 turn anticlockwise to give the right hand figure.

30 - 2
In each diagram, add the numerical values of the four letters and write the two digit answer down the right hand column.

31 - O
Starting top left and moving clockwise in a spiral, letters follow the alphabetical sequence, missing out letters written without any curved lines.

LEVEL ⑧

1 - 34
Working with the corresponding numbers in each box the numbers decrease by one each move downwards.

2 - P
In each row letters increase in value from left to right in steps of three for the top row, then 4, 5 and 6 for the other rows.

3 - 7
Splitting the diagram into four smaller squares the value in the box towards the centre equals the sum of the other three numbers.

4 - O
In rows, each letter is represented by a 2 digit figure, the first digit being the difference between the left and centre numbers, the second digit equals the sum of the two numbers.

5 - 3
Starting top left and moving clockwise in a spiral, the sequence of letters I, R, T, W, E, D, B, T, F, O, O, S repeats over and over.

6 - 10 metres.

7 - B
In each row, add the black squares from the left hand and centre boxes to give the figure in the right hand box.

196

8 - 6
For the first sequence, double the top numbers separately and enter the answer in the third box down, repeat this for the fifth line. For the next sequence add one to each figure on the second row and put the answer on the fourth row, repeating again for the last row.

9 - 10
Numbers are arranged in columns of 4, with each one increasing downwards in steps of 2.

10 - 17 & M
Numbers on the left descend in prime number order, starting with 3. Values of the right hand letters also follow the prime order sequence, this time starting with 2.

11 - 1600
She likes squared numbers.

12 -

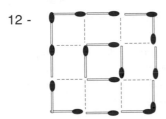

13 - 6
Take the 2 digit number at the centre of each segment putting the sum and the difference of the two digits in the segment opposite.

14 - 37
As you go down, double the previous number and subtract 5.

15 - 6
In each square, add up the outer three numbers, then add the two digits of the result together to give the central number.

16 -

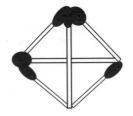

17 - 6
Each row and column contains 4 consecutive numbers in a random order.

18 - F
Starting bottom right and moving in an anticlockwise spiral, letters skip 1 space, then 2 etc. etc. returning to the letter A whenever Z is reached.

19 -

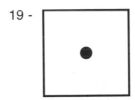

In rows, the right hand box contains only the features common to the two boxes to the left. The columns are calculated the same way, with the bottom box containing only the features common to the boxes above it.

20 - 12
In each triangle, divide the product of the upper and left hand numbers by the right hand number to give the central number.

21 - 3
Working in columns, subtract the middle number from the top number and multiply by 3 to give the bottom value.

22 - 3
In each diagram, add up the 4 outer numbers to give a 2 digit value. Add these 2 digits together to give the central value.

23 - 24
Square the numbers 1, 2, 3, 4 and 5 and subtract 1.

24 - D
The figures in the other three boxes total greater than 100.

25 - O
Moving from left to right, letters on corresponding points of each triangle increase in steps of 4, 5 and 6.

26 - B
In each square take the numerical value of the left and right segments to give the value of the letter in the top segment and the reverse alphabetical value of the letter in the bottom segment.

27 - 8
For each number on the left, starting at the top, double it and subtract 1, then 2, 3, 4 etc. to give the right hand number.

28 - R
Starting on the left in rows, letters ascend in sequence at intervals of 5 for the top row, then 4, then 3.

29 - Jenny is 37, her father is 73.

30 - 14
The numbers in the inner ring are the same as the numbers in the opposite outer ring, divided by 3.

31 - 5
In rows, the sum of the left and centre value equals the right hand value for the first and third rows, in the second and fourth rows the right hand value equals the difference between the left hand and centre numbers.

32 - T
Add the reverse alphabetical values of the three letters around each triangle to give the middle letter in forwards alphabetical order.

33 - 6
In rows, the right hand figure equals the sum of the left and centre numbers plus 2.

LEVEL  9

1 - 29
In each star the central number equals the difference between the sum of the odd and even numbers.

SOLUTIONS

2 - 4
The sequence is subtract 2, then add 1, etc.

3 - Z
Going from left to right along the top line then the bottom, letter values increase by three while their positions move 90° clockwise.

4 - 43
In each circle, starting top left and moving clockwise, multiply each number by 3 and subtract 5 to give the next number.

5 - 161
In each circle, going clockwise, double the first number and subtract 1 to give the next number.

6 - E
The sum of the numbers gives the left hand letter, and also the right hand letter in reverse order.

7 - 6
The central number of each triangle equals the difference between the sum of the odd and even numbers.

8 - 3
The numbers in the central column equal the sum of the numbers in the same row to the left, minus the numbers on the right.

9 - 64
Each box represents the cube of numbers 1, 2, 3 and 4.

10 - N
In each square letters in opposite segments hold the same position in the alphabet running forwards as they do going backwards.

11 - 2
In rows multiply the far left number by the far right to give the 2 digit result, written in the central squares.

12 - N
The numerical value of each letter equals the product of the two numbers in the opposite segment.

13 - N Working in rows, letters advance by 4, 2 and 5 places.

14 - P
Starting top left and moving clockwise to end in the centre, the letters increment by a repeating sequence of 1, 2 and 3 places.

15 - 24
Working clockwise, numbers increase by 2, 3, 4, 5 and 6.

16 - B
Working in rows, invert the left and right hand boxes vertically and add the elements together to give the middle box.

17 - 2 and 9 of any suit.
Working in rows the sum of the numerical values of the first five cards equals the 2 digit number represented by the last two cards.

18 - E
Working in columns, top to bottom, one spot is removed in sequence at each step.

19 - 6
In each diagram, the central number equals the difference between the product of the two right hand numbers and the product of the two left hand numbers.

20 - X
Working left to right, starting on the top row, letters increase in value in steps of 2, 3 and 4.

21 - 39

22 -

Break two of the matches in half.

23 - 66
As you move clockwise double the preceding number and subtract 2.

24 - 19
Starting top left and moving clockwise around each square, numbers in corresponding segments advance by 2, 3, 4 and 5.

25 - 23

26 - Z
Going clockwise around each star increase in numerical values by 6, 7 and 8 spaces.

27 - K
The central number in each triangle equals double the sum of the numerical values of the letters on the triangles points.

LEVEL 10

1 - K
Starting at top left and moving clockwise in a spiral, letters move back through the alphabet in steps of 2, 3, 4, etc.

2 - W
Starting at the top, the value of the right hand letter is two ahead of the left hand letter, then 3 ahead, then 4, etc.

3 - 35
In each circle, multiply the two smallest even numbers and put the answer in the opposite segment, do the same for the odd numbers.

4 - 236
Starting at the top, numbers increase in steps of 25, 35, 45, etc.

5 - Y
In each circle opposite segments contain letters the same number of spaces in from the start of the alphabet as they are from the the end of the alphabet.

SOLUTIONS

6 - 26
In each square, multiply the three outer values and subtract the number in the centre. Going clockwise the answers are 50, 60, 70 and 80.

7 - 14
Working in column, alternately add 5 then subtract 1 as you move down.

8 - N
Starting at the upper circle and working downwards, letters in corresponding segments increase in value by 2 each time, while their relative positions rotate 1 segment clockwise.

9 - N
Letters are put in alphabetical order, working clockwise around each circle, and from left to right, missing out letters written with any curved lines.

10 - 7
Working from left to right, all digits increase by 2, with their relative positions rotating 1/4 turn clockwise.

11 - 10
In each square, take the sum of the odd numbers and subtract the sum of even numbers to give the number enclosed in the central square.

12 - V
In columns, make a 2 digit number from the numerical values of the top and middle letters to give the numerical value of the bottom letter.

13 - E
Working in rows from left to right, the * moves back and forth along a diagonal line, the ? moves 1/4 turn clockwise, the O moves clockwise by 1 space, then 2, then 3, etc. and the # moves left and right along the second row.

14 - F
In each circle add the reverse alphabetical values of the top two letters to give the reverse alphabetical value of the bottom letter.

15 - 8
In each figure the top left number divided by the centre number gives the top right number, as do the bottom left and right numbers.

16 - 8
Working in rows, the central value equals the product of the left and right hand numbers, minus their sum.

17 - P
The letter in the bottom segment of each square has the numerical value of the sum of the letters in the other three segments.

18 - W
Starting from the top left and going down, then from top right down, letters advance by 5, then back 2 etc.

19 - R
Letters in the right half of the circle are seven places in front of the opposite letters.

20 -

Slide the horizontal match 1/2 length to the right and move the lower left match to the upper right, inverting the glass and enclosing the coin.

21 - 86
Working from top to bottom, double the previous number and subtract 1, 2, 3 and 4.

22 - 1
Multiply the outer 4 numbers together and divide by 2 to give the central figure.

23 - 24
Starting at top left and moving in a uniform pattern, numbers increase by 8, 7, 6, etc.

24 - 11
In each column, numbers increase in steps of 3, 4 and 5.

25 -

The sequence is as follows:

Working from left to right, circles at the top of each triangle move backwards through this sequence, corresponding circles at the bottom move forwards through the sequence.

26 - N
Going clockwise, letters increase in steps of 1, 2, 3 and back to 1 again.

27 - 2
In each diagram divide the top left by bottom right, add bottom left and subtract top right to get the answer in the middle.

28 - 88
Moving downwards, multiply each number by 3 and subtract 14.

29 -

Working in rows starting on the left, one circle is removed in sequence as you move towards the right.

30 - E
The others all cover the same area.

SOLUTIONS

LEVEL 11

1 - 14
In each triangle the centre figure equals the sum of the two lower numbers minus the top number.

2 -
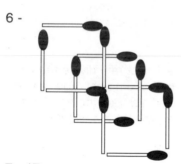

3 - 7
In rows the right hand number equals the difference between the left and centre numbers.

4 - 1
In each box, divide the 3 figure value represented on the upper line by the three figure value on the lower line. The answers are 22, 23 and 24.

5 - 4
Working in rows, the central value equals the sum of the squares of the left and right hand numbers.

6 -

7 - 17
Starting in the top left square and moving clockwise, numbers increase in sequence by 2, 3, 4 and 5, keeping their corresponding positions in each square.

8 - X
Starting at the top, letters increase in value by 5, 4, 3 and 2.

9 - C
From the top, using the first 2 digit figure, the left hand letter below equals the alphabetical value of this figure and the right hand letter below equals the reverse alphabetical value.

10 - 61
Starting at the top, double each number and add three to get the next one.

11 - B
If the watches are inverted, the digits read the same.

12 - D
Starting at the top left of the first figure and moving in a Z shape, letter values increase by 2, then 3, then 4, 5, and 6 to reach the top figure in the next diagram.

13 - 4
The number in the centre of each triangle equals the product of the bottom two digits, plus the top digit.

14 - 1
The grid is symmetrical around the two diagonal axis.

15 - D
Moving left to right along each row, the circle moves 3 places clockwise around the edge of the square, the triangle moves back and forth along the top left, bottom right diagonal and the star moves from the top to the bottom in a zigzag pattern.

16 - 1:02
Three is taken away from each column in turn.

17 - B
In each square, the outer letters advance the same number of spaces indicated by the numerical value of the centre letter.

18 -

21	4	15	24	1
6	8	17	14	20
3	19	13	7	23
10	12	9	18	16
25	22	11	2	5

19 - Five of Spades
Moving from left to right, cards are placed in alternate colours and suits, the red cards increase by two, the black cards decrease by two.

20 - 4
The numbers in the inner ring correspond to the number of lines used to make the letters in the outer ring.

21 - 24
Each number equals the sum of the two numbers above it.

22 - 2 of any suit.
In each row the sum of the even cards, minus the sum of the odd cards, equals 10.

23 - 14
Starting top left and going to the right, alternatively up and down, add 3 to each number.

24 - 3
In each circle the sum of the digits equals 30.

25 - Steve = 270, Simon = 540 and Stewart = 90.

26 - R
Starting at top left and moving clockwise in a spiral, letters increase by four each time.

27 - £6

28 - 22
In each row, add the left and right hand numbers and double the answer to give the central value.

29 - 13, 4, 15 & 9
All rows columns and diagonals add up to 34.

30 -
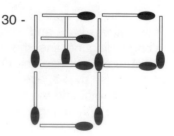

SOLUTIONS

LEVEL 12

1 - From top to bottom Seven of Clubs and Ace of Hearts.
Each suit has a value, Hearts = 4, Clubs = 3, Diamonds = 2 and Spades = 1, multiply the cards by its suit value and the sum of each row is 100.

2 -

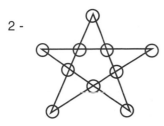

3 - 7
Each row and column contains each digit 0-9 inclusive, sometimes as part of a two digit number, sometimes alone.

4 - A = 92, B = 112
All other numbers are divisible by 3.

5 - 17
Taking the four segments at a time in vertical and horizontal lines, numbers increase by 2, 3, 4 or 5 for each line.

6 - S
Each line and column contains a letter made up of all straight lines, all curved lines or a combination of both.

7 - 6
Multiply the two outer numbers in each segment and divided by 2 then 3, alternately, putting the result at the centre of the opposite segment.

8 - 23
As you go down, numbers increase by 2, 4, 6 and 8.

9 - E
The numerical values of the letters in each column of 3 add up to 26.

10 - From top to bottom, King of Spades, Seven of Spades and Four of Hearts.
The sum of the two court cards equals the sum of the pip cards. There is one pip card of each suit in every row, plus an extra pip card of the same suit as the court cards.

11 - 3
The numbers in each row add up to 21.

12 - 35

13 - F
Starting on the outer left hand circle and going in a clockwise spiral, the letters are written in alphabetical order, missing out the vowels.

14 - 58
The sequence is multiply by 2, then add 3 etc.

15 - 15
In each star the sum of the even numbers, minus the sum of the odd numbers, equals the value of the number in the middle.

16 - Y
In rows, add the numerical values of the left and centre letters to give the value of the right hand letter.

17 - 23

18 - 7
In each diagram, multiply the top two numbers together, then divide by the lower right number and add the lower left number to give the central value.

19 - I
The sum of the numerical values of the left hand letters equals the value of the centre letter, as does the sum of the right hand letters.

20 - 33

21 - L
In each square, the total of the three numbers gives the value of the central letter.

22 - 11
Starting at the top left, and moving alternately right and left as you go down, add 2 to get the next value, then 3, then 4, etc. Follow the same pattern with the top right number but add 1, then 2, then 3, etc.

23 - 3:42am
The watch gains 16 minutes per hour.

24 - 2
In each circle, the letter is converted into its 2 digit numerical value. Add these 2 digits together to give the value in the opposite segment of the circle.

25 - 3
In each row, the sum of the squares of the far left and right numbers is entered in the middle two boxes.

26 - 18
Starting with the left group, the centre figure equals the sum of the left hand digits, the other groups follow suit but the positions of the outer numbers rotate clockwise 90° as you move to the right.

27 - 18
Add 2, 3 or 4 to the numbers in the left hand circle and rotate their positions 1/3 of a turn clockwise as you move along.

28 - 16
In each row, divide the left and right values by 3 and multiply together to give the centre number.

29 - 5
The numbers in the black segments are the difference between the numbers on either side.

SOLUTIONS

1 - D
Reading from the left, line by line, the @ moves in a figure of 8 around the corners, the * moves anticlockwise in steps of 2 around the 2 central columns, and the △ moves to and fro along the third row.

2 - E
The dots form a symmetrical pattern from top left to bottom right.

3 - 17
Moving diagonally downwards from left to right, numbers increase by the same amount each line.

4 - 10
The numbers in the top half of the outer ring are written in reverse order plus 1 in the inner ring and vice versa.

5 - 179
Moving clockwise, double the previous number and add 1, 3, 5, 7 and 9.

6 - E
Add all the digits on each watch together. All the others are square numbers.

7 - From top to bottom, Jack of Hearts, Seven of Clubs, Queen of Clubs and Two of Diamonds. The grid displays rotational symmetry 180° around the central Ace of Hearts, with the cards swapping to the other suit of the same colour.

8 - 3
In each triangle, multiply the bottom numbers to get a 2 digit number, add these together to get the top number.

9 - The figures pointed to by the hands add up to 10, therefore a number of options are available.

10 - 14
In the top pair of boxes the letters are rotated 90° clockwise and the corresponding numerical value is put in the segments on the right. The bottom pair of boxes follows the same rule but the reverse numerical alphabetical value is put on the box on the left.

11 - N
The number in the centre of each triangle equals the sum of the squares of the numerical values around each triangle.

12 - D
In rows, letters increase in numerical value by 3 as you move to the right.

13 - C & Y
Starting at the top of the first 2 columns and working down, each pair of letters is duplicated in the right hand columns from the bottom up with each letter advancing one place alphabetically.

14 - 14
The central value of 15 equals the average of the numbers on opposite sides of the diagram.

15 - L
Letters are arranged in pairs in opposite segments of the circle, the lower value letter is the same distance from the start of the alphabet as the other is from the end.

16 - R & H
Starting top left and working clockwise, move forward 6 places, back 2, then forward 4. etc.

17 - 13
In each row, multiply the first and second numbers, then subtract the third to give the value in the right hand box.

18 - J
Take each letter in the left half of the circle and add 5, put the result in the opposite segment on the right.

19 - 1
In each circle, multiply the top two numbers together to get a 2 digit number, add these together until you get a single figure number which goes in the bottom segment of each circle.

20 - 14
The sum of the left and right numbers equals the sum of the other three numbers.

21 - G
In each circle, going clockwise, letters move back 3 places, then forward 1, etc.

22 - 34 & 36
From top left digit add 2 to get the lower number. Add these together to get the next top number and continue for each column.

23 - 6
In rows, the centre number equals the sum of the left and right hand numbers, plus the central number from above.

24 - 22
Going clockwise, add 1, then 2, then 3 etc.

25 - V
Starting at the top, letters move forward by 2, 3, 4, 5 and 6 places.

26 - 3
The value in each lower box represents the sum of the squares of the two numbers directly above it.

SOLUTIONS

27 - 1 sheep.

28 - K
Add the numerical value of the top left and centre letters to give the lower left letter, similarly with the top right and centre letters to give the lower right letter.

29 - M
Moving down the column, advance 2 letters, then back 5, etc.

LEVEL 14

1 - S
Numerical values of the letters represent the first 10 prime numbers.

2 - 14
Starting top left and moving to the right, then down to the left, and finally down to the right, numbers increase by steps of 2, 3, 4 etc.

3 - 1 = Molly, 2 = Frank, 3 = Ray, 4 = Maude.

4 -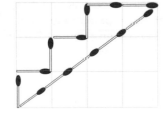

5 -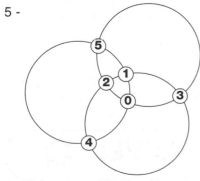

6 - Q
In each circle letters increase in value by 1, while their relative positions move 1/4 turn clockwise as you move to the right.

7 - I
Letters are written in alphabetical order, skipping letters written with curved lines.

8 - 52
Divide each number in the first circle by 2 and enter the new figure one place anticlockwise in the second circle. Multiply the first set of numbers by 2 and enter this figure one place clockwise in the third circle.

9 - Ace of Spades
In each row the value of the right hand card equals the difference between the sums of the red cards and black cards to the left. There is always 1 card of each suit on every row.

10 - A
If the separate digits on each watch are added together, the sum increases by 5 each step.

11 - 21
The numbers in each box equal the numerical values of the five vowels.

12 - 3
Working in rows, reverse the digits in the left and right hand shapes, then divide the new left hand value by the new right hand value to give the number in the centre.

13 - Three (Spades or Clubs)
In each row, add the values of the black cards to get a 2 digit number. Add these digits together to get the value of the red card in the middle.

14 - F
Starting with the letter at the top left, and moving clockwise around each triangle, letters increase in value by 2, 4, 6, 8 etc.

15 - T
In each row, the numerical value of each letter increases by 3 for the first row, 4 for the middle and 5 for the last.

16 - 5
Add the middle three numbers and write the answer, in reverse, in the first two columns. Multiply the same three numbers and write this answer, again in reverse order, in the last two columns.

17 - 4
Working in alternate rows, from left to right, numbers follow a repeating sequence of 5, 7, 2, 1, 9, 0, 3 and 6. The letters follow the sequence J, Q, L, C, Y, P, R, A, S.

18 - Eight of Clubs
In each row, the numerical value of the answer equals the average of the sum of even cards plus the difference of the odd cards. The suit of the answer equals the suit of the highest odd card in each row.

19 - 21

20 - The bottom line is the product of all the other numbers.

21 - 1
The square is divided into four 5 x 5 squares, each with the same pattern of numbers.

22 - Three of Hearts
In each row the average of the 3 cards to the left equals the value of the card on the right. There is one card from each suit on every row.

23 - 410
In all the other numbers. the first two digits added together give the third.

24 - 9:00pm

25 - From left to right - Four, Nine, Eight and Four (of any suit).

SOLUTIONS

In each column the sum of the top three cards and the sum of the bottom three cards equals the value of the central card.

LEVEL 15

1 - 12
Square each number in the inner ring and take away the original number. Write the answer in the outer ring opposite.

2 - 14
Taking the first two lines as one group starting top left and the bottom two lines as the second group starting bottom right and moving clockwise around each one, the first number in the top group is doubled to give the corresponding value in the second group, the next is halved etc.

3 - C
The sum of the separate digits on each watch add up to 18.

4 - Nine of Spades, Nine of Diamonds, Seven of Spades and Two of Spades.
In each row, spades represent positive numbers and diamonds represent negative numbers. The card on the far right of each row represents the sum of the cards to the left.

5 - 30
In each circle starting top left and going clockwise, double the first number and subtract 2 to give the next value.

6 - A
If viewed from the left edge the boxes show numbers 1-6.

7 - Eight of Clubs.
In each row, as you move to the right, the values increase by 2, 3 and 4 with each suit appearing once in each row.

8 - 41
Opposite sides of a dice add up to 7, giving 21 dots per dice. Multiply this by three and take away the dots you can see.

9 - 13
Going clockwise add 4 to get the next number, then subtract 2, etc.

10 - 37 & 45
In each square the central value equals the sum of the product of the top two numbers and the product of the bottom two.

11 - 27
Starting at the bottom left, move to the right diagonally up, then diagonally down etc. increasing the numerical value by 4 each step. Additionally the two figures remaining in each group add up to the centre figure.

12 - 1
The centre figure is the difference between the product of the top two numbers and the product of the bottom two.

13 - From left to right - Nine of Diamonds, Jack of Hearts, Six of Clubs and Queen of Hearts.
Starting at the top left, cards move clockwise in a spiral in the repeating sequence 2, 9, 5, Q, A, 3, 6, J, K. The suits follow the sequence H,C,H,S,S, D in an anticlockwise formation.

14 - Z
Starting at the top letters increase in steps of three for the left hand column and four for the right hand column whilst missing out all the vowels.

15 - 30
Numbers increase by 7, then 6, 5, 4 and 3.

16 - K
The centre figure equals the sum of the numerical alphabetical value of the left hand letter and the reverse alphabetical value of the right hand letter.

17 - 14
Starting on the left on the first group and moving up and down towards the right, numbers increase by 2 and 3. In the second group by 3 and 4 and in the third group by 4 and 5.

18 - 3
Moving from left to right, letters in the top circles increase in value from one circle to the next by the corresponding numbers in the circles below.

19 - L
Starting at the top of each triangle, letters move forward by three places going clockwise, ending in the centre.

20 - O
Taking the numerical values of the letters in the left hand circle, multiply them by two to give the values of the corresponding letters in the centre circle. Then multiply by three to give the values in the last circle.

21 - Z
In each circle, starting top left and going clockwise multiply the numerical value of each letter by 2 and then subtract 2 to give the next letter.

22 - 13
Going clockwise around the 4 boxes, the values in corresponding segments increase by 1, 2, 3 and 5.

23 - 4
The grid is symmetrical around the bottom axis running from top left to bottom right.

LEVEL 16

1 - 5
Taking the top two numbers to form a 2 digit number, subtract the 2 digit number at the bottom to give the central number.

SOLUTIONS

2 - Eight of Clubs
Moving from left to right, card increase in value by 2, 3, 4, 5 and 6, returning to Ace whenever the King is reached and always following the same suit pattern.

3 - 5
Numbers in the bottom left circle equal the sums of the numbers in corresponding segments in the upper left and centre circles. Numbers in the bottom right circle equal the difference between the numbers in the centre and right top circles.

4 - 14
In rows subtract 1 from the left and centre numbers and multiply together to give the right hand number.

5 - 3 & 3
The values of the segments in the top circle equal the sum of the corresponding opposite segments in the left hand circle. The values in the bottom circle equal the difference between corresponding opposite segments of the left hand circle.

6 -
Janine £1.01, £100.10 & £121.11, Jackie £4.02, £49.07 & £169.13

7 - E
Starting with Y, letter values decrease by 2, 3, 4, 5 and 6.

8 - 1
The grid displays rotational symmetry of 180° around a central point.

9 - 39
Going clockwise, each number is doubled then subtract 1, then 2, then 3 etc.

10 - 6
Starting with each letter on the left, add 2 to give the number in the next two boxes, for the next groups add 3 and 4.

11 - 9
For each group, add first and second figures on the top row to get the final figure, and the difference between the first and second numbers for the bottom right box.

12 - Z
Working in diagonal lines from top left to bottom right, letters move forward by 4 places.

13 - 1
Numbers in the segments on the right hand half of the circle equal double the value of the numbers in the opposite segments, minus 3.

14 - 6
In each diagram the reverse numerical value of each letter is written in the box below plus 5 for the first diagram, 4 for the second and 3 for the third.

15 - 4:30
Multiply the hour value and minute value to give 36.

16 - 14
In each square the centre figure equals the difference between the sum of the left and right segments and the sum of the top and bottom segments.

17 - B
Working from left to right the square moves 2 segments anti-clockwise, the circle 3 segments anticlockwise, the star by 4 segments anticlockwise and the triangle 1 segment clockwise.

18 - From top to bottom, Black Jack, Red King, Red Four and Black Eight.
In the first five rows the sum of the red cards equal the value of the right hand card. In the first 5 columns the sum of the black cards equals the value of the bottom card.

19 - 142 - 3 = 139

20 - L
Going clockwise in each square, letters increase in value by the same amount.

21 - A
The figures are groups of three of the same number squashed and rotated 90°.

22 - 2
Moving from left to right each box contains a decreasing square number, minus the root. (7 x 7 = 49 - 7 = 42 etc.)

23 - 16
Starting with the top value and moving clockwise, numbers move around a 24-hour clock, advancing 5 hours for the left star, 6 for the middle and 7 for the right.

24 - From left to right -
Working in columns add the number of black segments in the first two circles to give the bottom circle. The third circle down is the difference between the first two circles.

25 -

26 - 1
The product of the first row gives the first number in the second row. The sum of the numbers in the top row gives the second number. Repeat this for rows three and four.

27 - From top to bottom, 14, 17 & 33.
Starting at the top and working in diagonal lines from left to right, numbers increase in value by 2, then 4, then 5 etc.

SOLUTIONS

LEVEL

1 - 3
The numbers in each row add up to 52.

2 - 36
The answer in the centre of each triangle equals the difference between the top and left hand values, multiplied by the right hand value.

3 - 63
The sequence follows the cubes of numbers 1, 2, 3 and 4, minus 1.

4 - 138
Starting bottom left and moving in a clockwise spiral, double the last number then subtract 5 etc.

5 - W or E
Moving clockwise, each segment contains an example of a letter written with 1 continuous line, 2 lines, then 3, then 4.

6 - Q
Moving clockwise letters advance in steps of 9, 7 , 5, 3 and 1.

7 - X
Starting top left, add 4 to get the box below, add 5 for the second column and 6 for the third.

8 - 3
Each row contains every digit 0-9 inclusive.

9 - 29
In each diagram multiply the top two values and add their sum to give the bottom value.

10 - W
Moving from left to right, top row then bottom, in each square, letters in the top left corner increase by 1 place, top right letters decrease by 2 spaces, bottom left decrease by 1 place and letters in the bottom right corner increase by 2 spaces.

11 - D
Working from left to right, symbols with curved lines move 2 places clockwise, whilst straight sided symbols move to the segment opposite.

12 - 5
Taking 3 x 3 groups of circles with a 9 in the middle, the figures 1 - 9 appear in every group.

13 - 3
In rows the sum of the numerical values of the two boxes are written as a 2 digit number in the two right hand boxes.

14 - J
The boxes follow the sequence of letters missing out those written with just straight lines.

15 - C
Add the digits in the minutes position to get the hour value.

16 - B
Working from left to right, the X moves clockwise 1 segment, then 2, then 3 etc.the △ moves clockwise 4 segments, then 3, then 2 etc. The ◯ and □ move to opposite segments and back again. A # and * fill the first two consecutive empty segments in a clockwise direction, and the • fills any segments left empty.

17 - A = 4, B = 6. Multiply the numbers on the second and third rows and write this answer along the top row, then multiply together the numbers along the top and write their squares along the bottom row.

18 - L
Moving from left to right, letters advance in steps of 1, 2 and 3 with their relative positions moving 1/3 of a turn clockwise each time.

19 - 2
Add the numbers from the top row to the numbers in the second row to get the third.

20 - 169
A descending sequence of the squares of prime numbers.

21 - 36
The first box shows the sequence of prime numbers. The second box multiplies these numbers by 2 minus 2, the third multiplied by 3 minus 3.

22 - 17
Going clockwise the numbers are the first 6 prime numbers plus 4.

23 - 4
The centre letter has the reverse alphabetical value of the corresponding left and right digits in each row when taken as a 2 digit number.

24 - £1

25 - 7
The sum of the 4 lower points minus the number at the top equals the number in the middle.

LEVEL

1 - 15
Top row follows ascending sequence bottom left to top right, plus 5 for the first group, 6 for the second and 7 for the third. Subtract top middle from bottom left to give bottom middle and add top left to give bottom right.

2 - 8
Letters in the top row are the same distance from the front of the alphabet as the corresponding letters in the bottom row are from the end of the alphabet. The figures in the middle row are half the numerical value of the letters in the bottom row.

3 - 1
Each number equals the square of the odd numbers in descending order from 11.

4 - C
Going clockwise letters move back 6 places then forward 2 places, etc.

SOLUTIONS

5 - 14
Multiply the two outer digits in each segment and divide by 2. This result is put at the centre of the segment 2 places clockwise.

6 - Seven of Diamonds & Eight of Spades.
The cards are arranged alternately in two sequences, one increases in steps of two, the other deceases by one. The suits follow the order Hearts, Diamonds, Spades Clubs.

7 - Three of Clubs & Nine of Hearts.
Taking the first five cards in each row, add the values of the odd cards to give a 2 digit answer. Add these 2 digits together to give the value of the club card in that row. Do the same with the even cards to give the value of the Heart in that row.

8 - 72
In the top circle, numbers in the upper half are multiplied by 3 and the result put in the segment opposite, in the left hand circle numbers are multiplied by 6 and by 9 in the bottom circle.

9 - F
Moving in rows from left to right, the row of dots at the top moves down 1 row each time, returning to the top when it reaches the bottom. The left hand column moves back and forth across the box. In addition, one dot starts in the bottom left corner and moves clockwise corner to corner and another dot fills the central space each time, however, should a black dot already fill either of these two places as a result of earlier instructions then the dot is left white.

10 - 20
In each circle, multiply the top two numbers together and subtract the lower right number to give the lower left number.

11 - 67
As numbers go down multiply by 2 and subtract 3.

12 - D
On each watch the minutes value equals the hour value multiplied by three.

13 - B
Starting top left and working to the right in each row, the top and third dot remain stationary, with the dot in between moving to and fro along its line 3 spaces at a time. The lowest dot moves to and fro 1 space at a time and the dot above it 2 spaces. The whole grid rotates 90° clockwise at each step.

14 - 10
In each circle the top right number equals the average of the left hand numbers and the lower right equals the difference between these numbers.

15 - M
Letters descend in reverse alphabetical order in intervals of 7 then 6, 5, 4 and 3.

16 - 21
In each circle, starting top left and moving clockwise, multiply the first number by 3 and subtract 3 to give the next value.

17 - A
Divide the minutes on each watch by 4 to give the hour value.

18 - 13
Starting on the left, values in corresponding segments of each circle increase by 1, 2, 3 and 4. The relative positions of the sequence rotate 1/4 turn clockwise as you move to the right.

19 - 2:53
Taking the hour and minute values separately, the hours decrease by 3, 4, 5 and 6 hours and the minutes increase by 21, 23, 25 and 27.

20 - 1
The figure in the centre of each triangle equals the sum of the squares on the three corners.

21 - 5
Working from left to right in each figure, the numbers add up to 32, 34 and 36.

1 - 9
Take each number in the outer ring as a 2 digit number and multiply them together. Write this answer plus 1 in the inner segment opposite.

2 - 12
In each box, square the top numbers and subtract 4 to give the lower number.

3 - 51
Starting from the left hand circle, working top to bottom in columns then to the next column to the right, add 1, then 2, then 3 etc. until the central circle, then subtract 11, 10, 9 etc.

4 - 56
In each diagram, divide the top left value by 3, multiply it by the top right value, then multiply the answer by 4 to give the lower value.

5 -

Working in rows, using the left hand figure as a source, reflect around a vertical axis to give the middle figure, and reflect around a horizontal axis to give the right hand figure.

6 - 55
The boxes follow the sequence of prime numbers multiplied by 5.

7 - J
In rows the left hand number equals the numerical value of the centre letter plus 1, the right hand number equals the reverse alphabetical value of the letter plus 1.

SOLUTIONS

8 - 19
In each row, starting on the left, multiply the number by 3 and subtract 2 to give the next number on the right.

9 - H
In each row, add the numerical values of the left and right hand letters to give the reverse alphabetical values of the central letter.

10 - 65
Moving downwards, double each number and subtract 1.

11 - X
Letters increase in value down each column by 4 in the first column, 5 in the middle and 6 in the right hand column.

12 - 78
Moving downwards, add 1 to each number and double it to get the next number.

13 - L
Starting at the top and working inwards in a clockwise spiral, letters increase in value by 4 each time.

14 - 2:53
As you move right the hour value decreases by 1, 2, 3, 4 each step and the minutes increase by 11, 12, 13 and 14.

15 - 4
In each row the first and third numbers when read as a 2 digit number give the reverse alphabetical value of the centre letter.

16 - 9
In rows, the centre value equals the product of the left and right hand numbers minus the sum of the left and right numbers.

17 - £2.30
The first three spend a total of £27.60 on 12 of each item, therefore each tool = £2.30.

18 - F
Working in rows, add together the left and central diagrams to make the diagram on the right. If a black square appears in both of these columns it becomes white in the third box.

LEVEL 20

1 - C & N
Letters in the bottom row are 1 place lower than the corresponding letters in the top row, letters in the third row are 2 places lower than the second row.

2 - 2
The sum of the numbers in the top and bottom rows is put in the corresponding position in the second row, the difference between the top and bottom rows is put in the third row.

3 - V
Starting top left and moving clockwise in a spiral, letters move forward by 2 places, then 3, then 4 etc.

4 - 1
The numbers at the centre equal the numerical value of the letter in the opposite segment, if this value exceeds 9 the digits are added together to give a single digit answer.

5 - 72
Moving in a clockwise spiral, numbers are double the square of the first 9 numbers.

6 - 477
Starting with the top 3 digit number, square the central digit and add this to the original number to give the next number.

7 -

Working from left to right and using the left hand circle as a source, the middle circle shows the original and its reflection about a vertical axis, the right hand circle shows the original and its reflection about the horizontal axis.

8 - 6
The sum of the numbers in the lines of three going upwards equal the sum of the numbers in the lines of three going downwards.

9 - A = 7, B = 9
The difference between the first and third columns as a 4 digit number going down is written in the central column going down.

10 - 4
The sum of the odd numbers in each column equals the sum of the even numbers.

11 -

30 dots in each column.

12 - 2
Take the numerical value of each letter and multiply by the opposite to get the answer in the middle.

13 - N
Starting top left and moving diagonally upwards from left to right letters are repeated.

14 - 2
Cube the numbers in each column of the top grid and add the answers together. Write this answer going down the columns of the bottom grid.

15 - B
Cube the numerical values of the letters in the top grid and add the answers together. Write this answer in reverse order in the columns in the bottom box.

16 - D
The others are symmetrical.

17 - Y - C - P - M - I - T - D - Y - A
There are two chains of letters in use. The first goes diagonally upwards from left to right starting in the top left corner and appears on alternate lines. This chain contains every letter of the alphabet except vowels. The second chain starts bottom right and goes diagonally downwards from right to left and contains every letter of the alphabet.